the Night Before the Dawn

Copyright © 2014 by Brent Heatwole

the Night Before the Dawn
Self published
ISBN: 978-0692208274

All rights reserved

Contents

I *Introduction*

II *Jesus is not returning soon*

III *The seven churches in Asia*

IV *The church in Ephesus*

V *The church in Smyrna*

VI *The church in Pergamum*

VII *The church in Thyatira*

VIII *Four beasts*

IX *The Vatican*

X *The church in Sardis*

XI *The church in Philadelphia*

XII *The war of Gog*

XIII *The white horseman*

XIV *A new world order*

XV *The harbinger*

XVI *The night*

XVII *A new Constitution*

XVIII *The dawn*

XIX *The end*

XX *Conclusion*

I

Introduction

Dear Reader, I should begin with a couple confessions. I am not really a writer. I cannot promise you that this book is well-written. I ask you to look past this, because there are very good reasons for reading this book in spite of its author. I also confess that you may have been brought to this book by a bit of sensational advertising, either through word of mouth or the internet. Its not meant to over-hype the book. There are grave predictions in this book, and substantial reasons to back them up. Unless I'm just totally off (you'll have to read to judge for yourself), this decade will be the most eventful decade since the time of Noah's flood, and the most meaningful decade since the time of Jesus' crucifixion and resurrection. That's not a lie, and its not hype.

At this point you might be thinking I'm going to predict the end of the world, just like every other sensational interpretation of prophecy. Not at all. This book is about prophecy, but its not about the end times. And I do not believe the return of Christ will happen soon (relatively speaking). The next chapter will explain why. There are many other prophecies in the Bible besides those about the Antichrist and return of Jesus. There are many other events foretold in the Bible; diverse events on a singular timeline. You can jump to the back of the book, if you're that type of person, where I have a visual timeline. Much of it depicts past events, but connects them to biblical prophecy. Some of it depicts future events. It will give you a basic overview of the timeline I believe best represents biblical prophecy.

The immediate purpose of this book is to warn people. No, I'm not going to go around crying Armageddon. But does the world have to end for people to be in serious danger? I believe there are millions of Americans, and millions more outside of America, who are in serious danger. My hope is to give as many people as possible some forewarning of these events. I will also mix in some moral lessons as I'm going through the prophecies. Its not the immediate aim of this book, but there are some basic Christian principles that have been neglected, and some common false doctrines that get in the way of Christian truth. Take it as you will; you will probably find at least something to disagree with. I don't pretend to be infallible. I'm not a prophet. I only claim to have some understanding of biblical prophecy. I have studied them, but not purposely at first.

I began reading books like Revelation just merely as a curiosity. It is certainly mysterious, the things that are said in books like Revelation and Daniel. I heard the common interpretations. I generally agreed with the common interpretations for a while. I used to think the end was near, as many prophecy interpreters do. I also came across some unusual interpretations of prophecy. Somewhere along the line I had an epiphany. I woke up to the realization that the seven churches in Revelation have a much deeper meaning. You'll see as you read this book what I mean about the seven churches. That began a journey of discovery, and from then on I looked at every prophecy as if it might have some profound meaning. I spent time meditating on certain prophecies. By the way, if you want to understand prophecy, meditation is the key. As you read this book, meditate on the things written.

I will always remember the day I discovered the meaning of the white horseman. To me it was huge. The feeling after having discovered something big, I cannot put it into words. Knowing that you know something; then after some research, finding out that basically no one else knows (to this day I'm not sure how many other people, if anyone, knew what I knew concerning the white horseman. Today I know at least some other people know, because I told them). I have had this feeling more than once. I have become convinced that its something from God. Either I'm just crazy, or time will prove there really is something to it. The other possibility is that I'm both right and wrong: right about some things, wrong about others.

So look it over. Look at the timeline in the back if you wish. Judge the cover if you wish. Then dive into the content. I can promise you, there is at least one thing in this book that you've never read or heard before. Even if you're well-read and highly educated, and you've read every book on prophecy there is, there will still be something new for you in this book. If you love things that make you think, continue.

II

Jesus is not returning soon

To contrast this book with other books on prophecy, let me start by saying that I do not believe Jesus is going to return soon. Many of my Christian brothers and sisters would disagree. They would point to things going on around the world as evidence that Jesus is going to return soon. I see it all the time. And I can't blame them, since the world seems frightful. Its hard to make sense of a nation that plummets further into immorality. The decline of morality, the increase in globalization, the advance of technology, all seem to point to the end of the world. But I believe they are mistaken.

The popular view in Christianity is that there will be a seven year tribulation period in which the Antichrist rules the world. Some believe Christians will be raptured before, during or after this period, and some believe the idea of a rapture to be false. But just about every Christian agrees that there will be a tribulation period, and that Jesus will return at the end of that period to restore the world to a righteous order. I myself do not see anything wrong with that view. I only disagree with many Christians as to when it will happen. Many like to say it will happen soon. I realize that much of it is just an attempt to frighten people into repentance. It is a "time is running out, get right with God", and "Jesus could return any moment, so be ready" kind of approach. Yet we need not think that Jesus could return at any moment to think our time on earth might be up at any moment. We should be ready to "meet our maker" any moment; not because He will return at any moment, necessarily, but that we can die at any moment, by any number of ways.

The tendency of people, when talking about prophecy, is to jump straight to the Antichrist, rapture, tribulation and second coming. It seems that prophecy and eschatology (study of the end times) are synonymous; that eschatology is prophecy and prophecy is eschatology. Eschatology is prophecy, but prophecy is not always eschatology. It is a mistake to think that all prophecy concerns the second coming of Jesus. And I believe it is a mistake to always jump to that subject. What you will find in this book is not a study of end times prophecy. You won't see me saying, "Jesus is going to return any moment," or any of the things you usually hear. I will talk about judgment that is coming soon. I will talk about our need, and the need of many people outside the US, to get right with God. But its not about the end of the world. A title like "The Night Before the Dawn" implies two things: a night, and a dawn. The night is what we see in the world today, as well as certain judgments from God that I believe are coming soon. The dawn is a new era in human history, which represents hope and joy. The corruption you see today, that is the night. But God is not done with the church age yet.

So why do I believe the second coming of Jesus is not soon? There are a number of reasons:

1. The most obvious is the fact that so many Christians believe He is coming soon. Jesus says that His coming will be like the days of Noah; hardly anyone knew the flood was coming, only Noah and his family. Jesus says that people will be eating, drinking, marrying and being merry right up until the end. Why?

Because they know nothing about it. The fact that so many Christians believe Jesus is coming soon is one good reason to believe Jesus is not coming soon, because it contradicts the prophecies concerning the time leading up to His second coming.

2. Paul prophesies a great apostasy in the last days in 2Timothy 3 and 2Thessalonians 2. He calls it a "rebellion". He says the man of lawlessness (the Antichrist) will set himself up in God's temple. The whole idea of apostasy is a turning away from the truth. An apostate Christian is someone who was a Christian but turned away from Christ. What Paul describes is the whole world in such a condition. A world that was Christian but turned away from Christ. As the world is today, that condition is impossible. I'm not saying things aren't bad; there's certainly a lot of evil in the world. But for the world to experience apostasy, it would have to be Christian first. And the whole world has not become Christian yet.

3. A third temple is mentioned, both by Paul and by John in Revelation. John writes the book of Revelation about 95 AD, which was 25 years after the temple in Jerusalem had been destroyed. Yet we find a temple in the prophecies of Revelation, indicating that a third temple will be built. Given that a third temple has yet to be built, we have one more reason to think Jesus' return is not soon.

4. Jesus says that the gospel will go out to all the nations before He returns. Some may think it means that the gospel touches a nation, as if one missionary proclaiming His word is enough to fulfill the prophecy. I disagree. I believe the gospel will actually saturate the world before He returns.

There's one prophecy and one parable, which is also a prophecy, that supplement this prophecy to help us understand it. There is a prophecy in Daniel 2, which talks about a mountain and a rock cut out of that mountain, but not by human hands (meaning God did it). Its in the context of Nebuchadnezzar's dream, which is a great statue with four layers. The layers of the statue pertain to four ancient empires: Babylon, Persia, Macedon (Alexander the Great) and Rome. But more important than the layers are the mountain and rock. The mountain represents the kingdom of Israel. The rock that is cut out is the church of Christ. The prophecy says the rock hits the statue on the feet (the Roman Empire) and then grows into a mountain that fills the earth. If it grows into a mountain that fills the earth, then the church of Christ will fill the earth someday. Not just touch all the nations, but fill them.

Second is the parable of the yeast and the dough. Jesus says the kingdom of God is like yeast that a woman took and worked it all throughout the dough. The yeast is the word of God. The dough is the earth. If the yeast is worked all throughout the dough, then the word of God will be worked all throughout the earth (I love the analogy). Not just touch every nation, but thoroughly worked through every nation. Has the gospel - the word of God - been worked all throughout the earth? Has the mountain - the church of Christ - filled the earth? No. So neither of those prophecies have been fulfilled; and in the context of those prophecies, Jesus' prophecy about the gospel going out to every nation on earth before the end hasn't been fulfilled either.

"But wait," someone will say, "didn't Jesus say He is coming soon?" Yes He did, but to whom did He say it? He clearly didn't say it to the Christians living in the first century. It certainly was not meant for them, otherwise Jesus would have lied. And if Christians in the first century believed Jesus was going to return soon, they were mistaken. The idea of Jesus returning soon seems to be so prevalent amongst Christians. It seems that Christians automatically assume that its a biblical theme (that its axiomatic). They might be surprised to find out that its only recorded once in the Bible, and that in Revelation. Its Revelation 22:7, the only place where Jesus says He is coming soon. To whom is He saying this? Clearly He's not saying this to the apostles, or to those in the first century, since it was written at the end of the first century. Clearly He's not saying it to anyone living since the first century, because He hasn't returned yet. He must be saying it to those who will be living at that time - during the end times. We would be mistaken if we thought that every part of the Bible is addressed to us. Some parts specifically apply to certain generations and groups of people.

I would also point out that in one of Jesus' parables - the parable of the ten virgins - the issue is not the soon return of Christ. If the bridegroom had returned soon, all ten would have been fine. The problem was not Him returning too soon, but rather His late coming. Additionally, there is the prophecy in Matthew 24:48-51, where the wicked servant says, "my master is staying away a long time." This is another case in which the issue is not Jesus returning too soon, but rather later than people expect. Because his master is not returning as soon as expected, the wicked servant believes he can get away with immoral behavior.

"But," someone will say, "the master returns when he doesn't expect him to. Jesus returns like a thief in the night." This is true. He does return like a thief in the night for them. His return is like the days of Noah, meaning people do not see it coming.

But does that mean nobody sees it coming? Or that Jesus' return is like a thief in the night for everyone? Paul tells us in 1Thessalonians 5:4 that it won't be. Just after reminding the Thessalonian church that Jesus' return will be like a thief in the night, he points out that they will not be taken by surprise from it, for they are children of the light. The specific words to them were irrelevant, since Jesus didn't return in their time, but the principle applies both to them and to us. The point is, if we are children of the light, meaning we have knowledge and understanding of the prophecies, we will not be taken by surprise when Jesus returns (even though I do not believe He will return in your lifetime). So Jesus does not return like a thief in the night for everyone, only for those who do not have the light of understanding, which at the time of Jesus' return will be practically everyone.

We have to understand that there is more to prophecy than just the last days. And yes, prophecy does apply to our time, but it doesn't mean we're living in the last days. You will discover in this book that there are biblical prophecies applying to every time since the first coming of Jesus. And that there are biblical prophecies applying especially to our time. Once we get out of the habit of jumping straight to eschatology, we can truly understand the prophecies. For instance, there are two wars of Gog mentioned in the Bible. One is in Revelation and the other in Ezekiel. Yet its obvious, when you compare them, they're not the same event. Their context is vastly different, and the details of the events are different. The one in Ezekiel is pre-Armageddon (meaning it will happen before Christ returns), and the one in Revelation is post-Armageddon. Yet neither of them are Armageddon. Both of them happen at a completely different time than Jesus' return, and both are nonetheless important.

This just shows you how prophecy is vastly bigger than the return of Christ. The return of Christ is an important part, but not the only part.

III

The seven churches in Asia

If we are to understand the timeline of God's church, and how the church will someday fill the earth, we have to understand the seven churches in Asia. This is Revelation, chapters 2 and 3. In the literal sense, they were seven churches in seven cities in Asia Minor. The true meaning of the seven churches, however, is not literal. They have a typological meaning (they're figures representing something much larger than themselves).

The book of Revelation, which is a book of prophecy, would not have much use for these seven letters, if the meaning of the churches didn't extend beyond the literal. None of the literal churches still exist today. And many of the details within the letters couldn't possibly make sense if we didn't understand them beyond the literal. A persecution that only lasted ten days, for instance, would be a meaningless persecution. Jesus says that Satan will have some of them locked in prison. What's the big deal about being locked in prison for ten days? If its a literal ten days, why does He even need to mention it? Clearly, the ten days are not literal. Jezebel, in the letter to the angel of Thyatira, was dead for almost a thousand years at the time it was written. And do you think Jesus would warn the church in Sardis of His imminent return, if He did not return and the church in Sardis no longer exists? Reason demonstrates that there's meaning here beyond the literal. Why else would Jesus say, "he who has ears to hear, let him hear what the Spirit says to the churches"? Anyone can hear the literal, but only he who has ears to hear can hear the true meaning of the letters; that is, the inner ear of understanding.

So what do the seven churches represent? They represent the church of Christ at various stages in its history. They represent different church ages, you might say. Each church age has a spirit (angel). The angel of each church gives it a unique character. And that particular character shows up through the church, in the age when it is most prominent. That is not to say that these are strict church ages. One church does not end at the same time that another begins. Rather one will emerge while the previous church (or churches) fade away. The churches themselves are not ages, but make it seem like there are church ages, since they are set in chronological order. You might say that each church has its own age, but not necessarily of equal duration.

The letters are addressed to the angel of each church, but the people of the church - the church itself - do need to pay attention, because Jesus says, "he who has an ear, let him hear what the Spirit says to the churches." So while the beginning of each letter indicates that the letter is meant for the spirit of the church, the end of the letter indicates that its also meant for the church itself; that is, the people of each church.

The important point is to recognize that each church has a spirit; there is a difference between the church in Ephesus and the church after it, Smyrna, which may seem like an arbitrary difference. Ephesus does not end and Smyrna directly begin. They are not mechanical segments of a timeline. The one spirit fades as the next one emerges, so that each church is prominent during its own church age, but not exclusive. There is little to differentiate between the churches, if we need to have something mechanical, tangible or mathematical. But if we see the governing spirit behind each church, shown by its own unique character, then we can distinguish between the church in Ephesus and the church in Smyrna. Of course these two churches are the earliest of the seven churches, and being so distanced by time as we are, it may be harder to distinguish them than it is to distinguish Thyatira and Sardis, which are more recent in church history.

The prophetic part of the seven churches clarifies both the history and future of the Christian Church (as well as the present). It answers questions like why there are Protestant, Catholic and Orthodox distinctions among Christians. It describes, in a way that is more supernatural rather than merely physical, the progression of Christian history. The other part of the seven letters is what we can learn and apply to our own spiritual lives. For instance, we learn that, though it is poor, Smyrna is rich; and that, though Laodicea is rich, it is poor. We're forced to understand, because of the paradox, the kind of poverty and riches that Jesus is talking about: the one physical, the other spiritual. We also learn that Jesus approves of Ephesus' hatred for sin and false doctrine. He makes it very clear that they judge those who call themselves apostles, and He commends them for doing so. How contrary to our culture which remembers only one thing Jesus said: do not judge.

As I go through the seven letters to the seven churches, my first objective will be to explain the prophetic side of the letter. That will mean describing each church as it fits into the context of the other churches - the whole Christian Church. I'll then spend a little ink on the moral and spiritual significance of the letter, and how we can apply it to our daily lives.

IV

The church in Ephesus

This is the church of Christ during the first century of its existence. It is also known as the apostolic church, because it was led by the apostles. They had something we don't have: apostles. And we have something they didn't have: a well-established New Testament canon. We go to the Bible as the authority on truth; they went to the authors of the New Testament, the apostles themselves.

In this first century context of apostolic authority it was very important to know who was and who wasn't a true apostle. Some claimed to be apostles, but weren't. Notice how Jesus commends the church in Ephesus: "You have tested those who claim to be apostles but are not, and have found them false." This only makes sense in a first century context where apostleship is a real question. If someone claims to be an apostle today, we laugh at them. We know that an apostle is sent by Jesus Himself, and that none today are apostles. But in the day of Peter, Paul and John, if Joe claimed to be an apostle, his claim had to be taken seriously, and it had to be tested. First century Christians did this well and kept the faith of Christ pure.

But not everything was good for the first century church. Jesus gives them a rebuke: "You have lost your first love." When the church began they were speaking in tongues, Peter preached the gospel, there were healings and miracles, Paul teaching late into the night, and Philip baptizing eunuchs by the road (one that we know of anyway). As you can imagine, there was lots of excitement. It wasn't long before this that apostles walked and talked with Jesus Himself. Their love for Him was fresh, and it rubbed off on the brothers and sisters around them.

Jesus says to them, "remember the height from which you have fallen." They started at a spectacular height in regard to spiritual fervor and love for Jesus. But as the century wore on, the miracles became fewer, the excitement dampened, the apostles were killed, the memory of walking and talking with Jesus faded; their love for Him grew cold. Their faithfulness to Jesus went from a motivation of love to a more mechanical obligation to keep the doctrine and practices free of heresy and sin. Faithful nonetheless, but in a different way. Jesus asks them to remember the love, and to return to it. Not merely the cold and mechanical actions of a group that has the right doctrine, says the right things, hates sin and does good. There should be more: a real burning, a passion, a love for Him.

We see that fall from a great height in individual cases as well. Often a new convert has a certain zeal and excitedness concerning Jesus and Christianity. Its easy for us to think, here is someone who's on fire for Jesus. Yet its not about where we begin the race, its about where we finish. I'm sure you remember the parable of the sower and the seed. There are four different types of soil on which the seed falls, and the seed is of course the word of God. Each soil represents a different type of person, demonstrating how people respond to God's word differently. The soil type that describes this type of person is the shallow soil. He says that they receive the word immediately with great joy. Outwardly it looks as though this person is the most Christian of Christians. But since the soil is shallow, once the sun comes up, the plant withers and dies. They have not the root to withstand the long, sometimes torturous, sometimes mundane, Christian road. They start high but end with a dead faith.

This doesn't exactly describe the church in Ephesus, because they do persevere, they do remain faithful. The plant is not withered or dead. But what a height from which they have fallen! It teaches us the importance of improving our relationship with Christ (a spiritual marriage actually). Its better to start as the good soil, which does receive the seed but not immediately and not with joy, contrary to the shallow soil. It can reasonably be guessed that the good soil has questions about the seed (the word). That its road to receiving the seed is neither straight nor short. It may even receive the seed as a last resort. As Jesus said, those who fall on this stone will be broken to pieces. Its the finish that counts. The joy of the shallow soil did not equate fruit nor a long spiritual life. But the quiet understanding and perseverance of the good soil did produce fruit. So begin cold, but end hot. Begin as a skeptic, but take an absolute faith to your grave.

One other piece of practical help from this letter I briefly mentioned in the previous chapter. Jesus commends the church in Ephesus for being able to perceive a false teacher, and their hatred for everything false. Its important that I point this out, because many in our modern church culture take a vaguely opposite view. The popular thing today is not hate, but love. Whenever a person does or says anything that doesn't sound loving, someone might say, "what would Jesus do?" The implication is that you're not being loving enough. I like to remind them what Jesus actually did do. When traders were turning God's temple into a market, He overturned their tables and drove them out with a whip. When Pharisees were pretending to be righteous with their outward show of piety and rule-keeping, He called them hypocrites, sons of the devil and vipers (read Matthew 23).

Hate is actually an essential element of love. If you love good, you hate evil. If you love your team, you hate your team's rival. If you love God, you hate Satan, the father of lies; and you hate deceit itself. So it was with Ephesus; they hated lies. They hated false doctrine. They hated the practices of the Nicolaitans (sexual immorality). And they were slow to believe it when someone called himself an apostle. All of it commendable.

V

The church in Smyrna

The church in Smyrna represents a wonderful time in church history. It was when Christians were being thrown to the lions, crucified, tortured, imprisoned and beheaded (and the list of gruesome things done to Christians goes on). Yes, I did say wonderful. While Christians were being martyred, the church was growing because of it. Tertullian wrote in his 'Apologeticus' that "the blood of the martyrs is the seed of the church". Jesus encourages them with these words: "Be faithful, even to the point of death, and I will give you the crown of life." They had life, even though they were given death on earth. They had riches, even though they were poor.

As you can imagine, Christians during this time were poor. Many Christians were slaves, or maybe you could say that many slaves were Christians. If they did have any wealth, someone would accuse them of being a Christian (illegal in the Roman Empire) so that they could confiscate their wealth. But Jesus says, "you are rich!" He means this in a spiritual way. They have wisdom, they have love, they have faith. They are rich in these spiritual gifts. James 2:5 says that God has chosen those who are poor to be rich in faith. Their riches are a heavenly sort, while on earth they are poor.

What does it mean that they will suffer persecution for ten days?

The ten days are symbolic; they represent ten periods of persecution. Christian tradition holds that there were ten major persecutions in the early period of the church, each one signified by the emperor in charge. They are as follows:

1. Nero, 67 AD: It is believed that Nero ordered the city of Rome to be set on fire. However the fire happened, Nero was blamed for it, and to shift the blame, Nero blamed the Christians. He had Christians tortured and killed in the most cruel and barbaric ways. It was then that both Peter and Paul were martyred in Rome.

2. Domitian, 81 AD: This is when a law was made that if anyone brought before tribunal confessed to being a Christian, he would be punished. It gives a real meaning to idea of "confessing" one's faith in Christ. Its also when the Apostle John was thrown in boiling oil. However, they could not kill him, so they banished him to the island of Patmos instead, where he wrote the book of Revelation.

3. Trajan, 108 AD: Here we have a letter from Pliny the Younger, governor of Bithynia (Roman province in northern Asia Minor), detailing some of the customs of Christians and lamenting the persecution against them. At this time some were crucified, crowned with thorns and speared on a cross, in imitation of Christ's Passion.

4. Marcus Aurelius, 162 AD: Some famous martyrdoms come from this time: Polycarp, Blandina, Justin Martyr, to name a few.

5. Severus, 192 AD: At this time Christianity had grown quite large and pagans were fearful of the success of Christianity. They prevailed upon the emperor and persecution ensued. A few martyrs from this time were Irenaeus, Leonidus, the father of Origen, Perpetua and Felicitas, whose stories are told in Eusebius' 'Church History'.

6. Maximus, 235 AD: Christians were killed without trial and dumped onto heaps, fifty or sixty together without the least decency.

7. Decius, 249 AD: Eusebius writes that this persecution had a purging effect on the church of Christ. Pride had divided the churches, and preachers were at odds with each other because of pride. Christianity had grown popular and the emperor was jealous of its success, so he tried to rid the Empire of Christianity.

8. Valerian, 257 AD: When one of the martyrs during this time, Lawrence, was demanded to show the church's treasure, he showed the prefect of Rome the poor children the church supported. At that the prefect grew angry, expecting the church to have physical wealth; and he had Lawrence killed.

9. Aurelian/Maximian, 274/286 AD: In 286 AD a legion consisting entirely of Christians was ordered to take an oath to assist in the extermination of Christians in Gaul. The legion refused, and the emperor had every tenth soldier killed. Still they refused, and he again had every tenth soldier killed, thinking this would cause them to recant. They remained faithful, and the emperor had every one of them killed by sword.

10. Diocletian, 303 AD: This was the final and greatest of the ten persecutions. Churches and books were burned, leaders were imprisoned and tortured, and finally Christians were ordered to be exterminated throughout the empire. This only inflamed the passion and faith of the Christian church.

I'm just giving you a brief overview of the period. To get a better idea of the things that happened, and all the glorious martyrs of the time, Eusebius' 'Church History' and John Foxe's 'Book of the Martyrs' are good reads. The Book of the Martyrs includes martyrs long after this time, many during the Reformation period, but is a concise record of the martyrs.

The church in Smyrna teaches us something profound: the truth of humility. The invincible reality that God's humble servants are in fact kings and queens. That it doesn't matter what your station in life is; it only matters how God sees you. And God doesn't see everyone the same. Its true, He doesn't play favorites on the basis of wealth or race or anything worldly. But He does play favorites on the basis of who is most faithful to Him, against those who are inclined to compromise the truth. I think the letters themselves show that. The church in Smyrna is one of God's favorites. They aren't rich, nor are they appealing in any material or worldly sense. But they are humble. They do submit to God, even to the point of death. They don't think they know better. They don't question God's directives, but humbly accept their fate. They don't become angry with God because they are poor and suffer. So many today think they have a justified excuse to be angry with God, or to deny that He exists, because of some trouble in their lives. But these saints in Smyrna had as much trouble as any person could, yet they never blamed God or had contempt for Him. They had nothing but love and humble submission towards God.

It also teaches us that life is a lot more than money. My generation especially needs to hear some hard truth concerning this. We are raised in a culture that worships wealth. It seems that our culture can find no purpose or meaning in life, so we just go running after things that give us some momentary pleasure, even if its completely shallow. Thereby we end up living our lives for a buck and whatever pleasure we can find in a moment. Its no wonder then, all the social issues we have in America. Men don't want to get married, but just have easy sex. Women don't want to be mother and housewife, believing it will take away their independence. In both there is a selfish attitude which seeks personal pleasure, even if its at the expense of other people. But we find heartache at the end of the road. We seek what we think is good, but we destroy our relationships, hurt other people, and find that all of our pleasurable experiences are empty. We try to find meaning in materialism - careers, titles, pleasure and fancy things - but its just a house of cards.

The church in Smyrna, however, did not have this problem. They were singing hymns even at the point of death. We find a lighthearted joy in their writings. We find their love for other people, and especially other saints of the church, to be profound. And their love for God to be more profound still. Nothing could deter them. Their meaning in life was not shallow or material; it was eternal, deep and lofty. Their passion and resolve proved it. What's more, if you read about the martyrs, you'll find so many unique stories. Stories of supernatural events. Stories of self sacrifice. Stories that reveal the highest virtue and nobility in these poor saints. Though poor, though slaves, they literally do have mansions in the sky. Nobody today in our materialistic meaningless existence can touch that.

VI

The church in Pergamum

The spirit of the church in Pergamum emerged at about the time of Constantine. With the Edict of Milan in 313 AD Christianity was finally granted legal status. It did not become the official state religion until 380 AD. But from the time of Constantine onward, the Christian church in the Roman Empire was absorbed in Roman culture and religion, and there was a mixing of pagan and Christian belief. The strict adherence to orthodox doctrine that we saw with the apostolic church was waning, and there came to be a general acceptance of doctrine and practice that were not entirely true or Christian. Jesus says to them, "you have people there who hold to the teaching of Balaam," and, "likewise you also have those who hold to the teaching of the Nicolaitans." He's saying there are heretics in and among them. Balaam symbolizes false prophets and false doctrine; the Nicolaitans symbolize immoral behavior.

The first part of this letter is very interesting. He is commending them for their faithfulness, while at the same time seeming to give a rebuke for where they live. The church has remained true to His name, even in the days of Antipas. Persecution against Christians lingered, even after the Edict of Milan. Although, since Jesus is addressing the spirit of the church in Pergamum, and that spirit was emerging around the time of Constantine, it could be that Jesus was commending them for being true to Him during the time of Diocletion's persecution. And it is was in their city where Satan lives, the text tells us. What city? Not Pergamum literally, but where the actual church of Pergamum took up residence. That was the Roman Empire. Since the Roman Empire granted Christianity legal status, even though other parts of the world, like Persia, were still persecuting Christians, and since Christianity became the official state religion of the Roman Empire, it can be said that this church lived in Rome. The Roman Empire was their shelter in a way. And the place where Satan has his throne? There is one other place in Revelation that mentions the throne of Satan. It is clear that the dragon in Revelation 12 is Satan, and in Revelation 13:2 it is said that the dragon gave the beast, which is the Antichrist, his power and his throne. So we know that the Antichrist will possess Satan's throne. Revelation 17:7 says this beast - the kingdom of the Antichrist - has seven heads, and 17:9 says these heads represent seven hills on which the woman sits. Rome is known as the city on seven hills. So it makes sense that the woman in Revelation, which is figuratively called Babylon, is Rome, and there is where Satan has his throne. There is where the Antichrist will establish his capital.

So when does the church in Pergamum end and the church in Thyatira begin? The church in Pergamum sort of grows into the church in Thyatira. They are very similar. In both there is faithfulness; in one faithfulness in martyrdom, and the other faithfulness in hard work. In both there are false doctrines and immoral practices. In Pergamum the false doctrine and immoral practice is a general thing; its simply mixed in the church. But in Thyatira there is a specific source for the false doctrine and immoral practice: a woman named Jezebel. Sometime around the dark ages the old Catholic Church evolved into what is known as the Roman Catholic Church. We might say the transition happened sometime between 700 AD and 900 AD.

As for what can be learned from this letter, it is a rebuke on compromise. Their fault was that they tolerated heresy among them. They allowed false doctrines to creep into the church, and to intermix with true doctrine. Today people love to talk about being tolerant. But tolerance is a tricky thing. Of course we don't want to be like James and John, who asked Jesus if they should call down fire from heaven in judgment. Its not our place to condemn people in that way. However, we *should* make judgments about people, particularly concerning their teaching. We have to. The Bereans were commended for doing so, and it was Paul whose words they judged. If we tolerate heresy in our churches, then we have committed a sin against God. Hardly anything is worse than propagating a lie. These letters make it clear: false doctrines are very destructive, and God will judge those who willfully spread such falsehoods. So we have to be aware of the beliefs that are being spread among us. We must not tolerate any that go against God's word.

This brings me to another important point: the difference between a sinful act and sinful thinking. So often in our churches we simply think of sin as an act. As in, I committed a sin when I disrespected my parents (or something similar to that). But this doesn't really cover the issue of sin. Sin comes from the heart; its not simply an act. There are good and righteous saints who might on occasion accidentally sin, but do not have sin in their hearts. They are not sinners in the heart, but rather accidental sinners of the flesh. A person who is a sinner in the heart is someone who hates God. Its someone who loves sin; its someone whose sin comes from the heart. It shows in their deceptive teaching. The reason false doctrine is allowed to persist in our culture, and too often in our churches, is that people love lies more than truth. The lies are there to justify another one of their loves. Some love for pride or love for pleasure, the lie allows them to have. So there is no intention in their hearts to seek the truth, but only an intention to keep spreading lies. False doctrine is the evidence of people who have sin in their hearts. It is a sin that is more damning than the outward sinful act. As Scripture says, Satan is the father of all lies. The worst lies are the ones that take us away from understanding God's word. Should we as Christians tolerate it? Not at all! We should fight against it with all the strength we have. Let us remember that to fight against false doctrine in our day, we must have a good understanding of the Bible.

VII

The church in Thyatira

The church in Thyatira is the Roman Catholic Church. It is also the Eastern Orthodox churches. They work hard, and do many good things. Just look at all the schools, hospitals, monasteries, cathedrals, etc., they have built and established over the years. Jesus says about them, "I know your deeds, your love and faith, your service and perseverance, and that you are now doing more than you did at first." The church has progressed in doing more as it has grown. However, they tolerate a wicked entity figuratively called Jezebel. Jesus says that she calls herself a prophetess, and in verse 23 He speaks of her children, so we must consider her a mother. What do Catholics call "mother church"? The Vatican.

There's one major reason Catholics cannot be speaking of the church of Christ when they say "mother church": the church of Christ is not a mother. The church of Christ is only referred to in the Bible as a virgin pledged to be married to Christ. And the church cannot be mother of the saints, because the saints *are* the church. So when Catholics talk about "mother church", they are not talking about the church of Christ, even if that's what they think they're saying; they are talking about the woman Jezebel - the Vatican. The pope is called the "Holy See" and "Vicar of Christ", as if he can speak on behalf of Jesus. Remember, Jezebel calls herself a prophetess. The reformers called the pope the Antichrist, and they weren't far off. The pope is not actually the Antichrist, but he represents the woman Jezebel, and she is an antichrist, as when John speaks of many antichrists.

It may be worth the time to cover some of the Vatican's false doctrines. It begins with their claim to authority. They say apostolic authority is passed down in succession. No one disagrees that the apostles had authority. They had authority given to them by Jesus Himself. So whatever an apostle said, it is true. Yet none of the apostles said anything of their authority being passed down. To believe apostolic succession, you have to believe that the pope has authority, because it is based on the pope's word. But without apostolic succession, the pope does not have authority. Their argument for authority is circular reasoning. It doesn't have any basis in Scripture; its not founded upon any actual authority.

The Vatican also teaches Theotokos. It is the belief that Mary is the "mother of God". They say this, of course, by the reasoning that Mary was the mother of Jesus, and since Jesus is God, Mary is the "mother of God". What a tragically wrong conclusion! Mary was the mother of Jesus in the flesh, but as it says in John 1:1, in the beginning was the Word. Jesus exists eternally. Jesus existed before Mary existed. Mary may be Jesus' mother in the fleshly sense, but in the true sense of Jesus' existence, He has no mother. Jesus is born of our Father in heaven. Period. But if we want to talk about a spiritual mother of Jesus, we would have to go to Revelation 12. The woman there (I won't digress with too many details here) is Israel, and it says that this woman gave birth to a son who will rule all the nations with an iron scepter. That is clearly Jesus. In fact, Israel is the spiritual mother of both

Jesus and His saints, because it says "the rest of her offspring" (speaking of those who hold to the testimony of Jesus). But to call Mary the "mother of God" implies that God has a mother, which is absurd, and it also implies that Mary is herself a goddess. One of the chief accusations against the Vatican is that it promotes Mary worship (idolatry). Its not without reason; the Vatican certainly does promote Mary worship.

Another false doctrine of the Roman Catholic Church is the doctrine of Transubstantiation. It states that the wine of Communion literally becomes the blood of Jesus, and the bread literally becomes the flesh, when a Catholic priest blesses it. In a way, its like they're sacrificing Jesus over and over. They base it off of John 6:53, where Jesus says, "I tell you the truth, unless you eat the flesh of the Son of Man and drink his blood, you have no life in you." They take it to be literal; as in, we have to somehow literally eat the flesh and blood of Jesus. And the Catholic Mass is how, as they see it, this is accomplished. But if they read on just a few verses ahead, they will see where Jesus says, "the Spirit gives life; the flesh counts for nothing. The words I have spoken to you are spirit and they are life." This helps us to understand what Jesus meant in John 6:53. It could not have been literal flesh, because Jesus tells us the flesh counts for nothing. Then He tells us that the words He has spoken to us are spirit and life. So the words are spiritual with a spiritual meaning, and the words themselves are life. But if we have no life in us unless we literally eat Jesus, then how can his words be life? You see, the flesh and blood of Jesus in John 6:53 is not literally flesh and blood, but rather the words of Jesus. Remember, John 1:14 tells us that the Word became flesh. So even in the flesh Jesus is still the eternal Word of God. His true existence is not flesh, but rather the spiritual Word. True life does not come from the flesh, but it comes from Him, the Word. That is why the Spirit gives life. Its why the flesh counts for nothing. And why His words are spirit and life.

Don't let this confuse you. I know it may be hard to understand, but the principle point is clear. If you have Jesus' words in you - meaning you know, believe and keep His words - then you have life in you, because Jesus' words are life. Do you keep Jesus' words? Then you have life. You don't need to eat Jesus. You don't need the literal flesh of Jesus. You simply need the words and the spirit of Jesus, which in John 6:53 Jesus figuratively calls flesh and blood.

The woman Jezebel misleads Jesus' servants into eating food sacrificed to idols. It shouldn't be hard to figure out what this is: the Catholic Mass and Transubstantiation.

Jesus says of the Vatican, "so I will cast her on a bed of suffering, and I will make those who commit adultery with her suffer intensely, unless they repent of her ways. I will strike her children dead. Then all the churches will know that I am he who searches hearts and minds, and I will repay each of you according to your deeds." So how and when is this going to happen? To answer that I have to take you, Dear Reader, on a detour. I wouldn't have to if it was just to answer the question. But there's more to it. Since the church in Thyatira is the Roman Catholic Church, and the woman Jezebel is the Vatican, its pertinent to describe how God's judgment will happen. It will have much relevance to any Catholic, especially those with close ties to the Vatican. It will serve as a warning to them.

Its not that I know all the details concerning God's judgment of the woman Jezebel. Rather I know one major detail: the tool by which God will bring about His judgment. Think about the time when God used Nebuchadnezzar to bring judgment on the nation of Israel, as well as the city of Tyre. What does God say about Nebuchadnezzar? That he is a tool and a weapon in the hand of God. That God is using him to bring judgment on these nations. I believe we will see something similar with the Vatican. God will use a world power to punish the woman Jezebel. And I believe I know what world power that will be. Thus the reason for the detour. We have to explore the meaning of the four beasts in Daniel 7 to understand how God will bring judgment on the Vatican.

VIII

Four beasts

There are four beasts mentioned in the seventh chapter of Daniel. To understand what they represent we have to compare them to the four kingdoms represented in the layered statue of Daniel 2. Nebuchadnezzar has a dream, and in it he sees a statue. It has a head of gold, chest of silver, belly and thighs of bronze, legs of iron and feet of iron and baked clay. Daniel interprets the dream for Nebuchadnezzar. He tells us that these layers represent kingdoms, and the first layer, starting at the head of gold, is Nebuchadnezzar and the Babylonian Empire. Its not hard to figure out the rest from there. Persia is the chest of silver, Alexander and his Macedonians are the belly and thighs of bronze, and the Roman Empire is the legs of iron. Yet this fourth kingdom would become divided, like the iron and baked clay, and it would be partly strong (like iron), partly brittle (like clay).

As I mentioned in the second chapter of this book, there is a side story within this prophecy. A rock is cut out of a mountain, but not by human hands; the rock hits the statue on the feet, the statue comes crashing down, and the rock becomes a mountain that fills the whole earth. The first mountain is the kingdom of Israel. The rock is the church of Christ. Since the first Christians were all Jews, they were "cut out" of the mountain. The rock hit the statue on the feet, meaning the church of Christ assaulted, in a spiritual way, the empire, and the statue came crashing down.

The Roman Empire fell, but the church lived on. The rock grew into a mountain that filled the whole earth, which means the church of Christ will someday fill the whole earth.

Many people will interpret the four beasts in Daniel 7 as having the same meaning as the four layers in Daniel 2. Meaning they think these four beasts represent the same kingdoms, Babylon, Persia, Macedonia and the Roman Empire. But this doesn't make any sense. Why would the same prophet give two different prophecies that have the same meaning? Is it really so important that it needs to be repeated? Here's what I think it is: the four beasts in Daniel 7 are similar to the kingdoms represented in Daniel 2, but not the same. There are parallels, but they are not the same kingdoms. The four layers represent kingdoms in the pre-Christ era, but the four beasts represent kingdoms in the Christian era. The four layers represent kingdoms in the Middle East and Mesopotamian area, but the four beasts represent kingdoms in Europe. The only overlap is the Roman Empire, which covered both the Middle East and Europe. There we have the pivot which shifts from Mesopotamia and Daniel 2 to Europe and Daniel 7: Rome.

The beast that looks like a lion

The first beast looks like a lion, and has wings like an eagle. Its wings are torn off, it stands on its hind feet like a man, and the heart of a man was given to it. A clue to the meaning of this is on the English Royal Coat of Arms. The lion often symbolizes royalty. Great Britain, during its years of greatness, had all the power and majesty of a lion. Its empire crossed the world; they used to say, "the Sun never sets on the British Empire." The wings could either represent the British colonies in general, or the 13 British American colonies in particular. If they do represent the American colonies, we know why the wings are the wings of an eagle. And you shouldn't have to wonder what it means that the wings were torn off. Whether the wings represent the British American colonies specifically, or whether they represent British colonies generally, Great Britain lost its colonies.

After its wings were torn off, it stood on its hind feet and the heart of a man was given to it. What that means exactly, I'm not sure. But it is interesting that since Great Britain lost its superpower status, it has become what some call a "soft power". That means it has an influencing culture. Besides the fact that it has exported its language to the world, the UK continues to make some of the most popular books and movies. Just think about the best fiction writers over the last couple centuries. Sherlock Holmes is British. Middle Earth came from Britain. Narnia came from Britain. Hogwarts came from Britain. Not to mention the man that CS Lewis called his teacher, George MacDonald. For whatever reason, Brits have a wonderful creative talent. Is that what it means to be given the heart of a man? I don't know, but the UK does seem to have a very human character. Pubs, inns, castles, palaces, and a monarchy that's still in place. I'm an American, so its hard for me describe the UK. But I know enough to know that its quite different from American culture. American culture is mechanical, materialistic, competitive, practical, efficient. We do things in mass. They do things in style. They hold to old traditions that are a large part of their identity as English (or Scottish or Welsh). Its hard to define, and especially hard for an American to define, but its evident that the British culture has something of a human character.

The beast that looks like a bear

The second beast looks like a bear. Its raised up on one of its sides. It has three ribs in its mouth, and its told to get up and eat its fill of flesh. For this we must go back to World War II, a time in history that relates to a number of prophecies in this book (as you will see). What European country do you think of when you think of a bear? What country is often associated with the bear? When Hitler invaded Russia, it is sometimes said that this awoke a sleeping bear (synonymous to awaking a sleeping giant). Russia is big and powerful; and with its wide expanse and cold winters, it has the ability to retreat further inland and outlast its enemies (this was done with Bonaparte and Hitler). Russia was not aggressive or expansionist before WWII; it was only after the war that the Soviet Union took over eastern Europe. Russia was just like a bear in hibernation before the war, and a bear coming out of hibernation after the war, hungry and looking for food.

So what might the three ribs in its mouth be? I believe they are three world leaders, Roosevelt, Churchill and Stalin, who met in Russia at the Yalta Conference. It was to discuss how Europe, and specifically Germany, should be divided up since the war was over. That fits with the chronology of the prophecy. At that time (WWII) Great Britain had already lost its wings (colonies), and presumably had already been given the heart of a man, so that much of the prophecy concerning the lion beast had already been fulfilled. The beast that looks like a bear had been told to awaken by the invading Germans, it has three ribs in its mouth at the Yalta Conference, and it eats its fill of flesh, which was the Soviet Union taking over the countries that surrounded it, particularly eastern Europe. As for it being raised up on one side, that is because the large majority of Russian people live on the western third of Russia.

The beast that looks like a leopard

The third beast looks like a leopard. It has four wings like a bird, and four heads. And it is given authority to rule. This one is a bit peculiar. It will not strictly follow chronology, because it is not simply one kingdom. It is actually four kingdoms; that is what the four wings represent. And the four heads represent the leaders of each one. The four kingdoms are spread out over a long span of time. Each of them German in one way or another. The first wing is the Holy Roman Empire, and its head is Charlemagne. The second wing is the German Reich, and its head is Otto von Bismarck. The third wing is the Third Reich, or Nazi Germany, and its head is Adolf Hitler.

Did you ever wonder why Nazi Germany was called the Third Reich? This is why. What are the two reichs before it ("reich" is German for "empire")? Its not just me saying this; Hitler himself would have told you what the previous two reichs were, had you lived in that time and asked him. They fancied themselves as following in the footsteps of Charlemagne and the Holy Roman Empire, as did Bismarck and the German Reich. Do you remember seeing in history class an eagle that stood atop the Nazi symbol with its wings spread out? That is the Reichsadler. It comes from the Roman standard. It was adopted by the Holy Roman Empire, and subsequently used by second and third reichs. It remains on the German coat of arms (not the Reichsadler itself, but a version of the eagle).

The part of this prophecy that doesn't follow the chronology are the first three wings (reichs). The first (Holy Roman Empire) came and went long before the lion beast (Great Britain) came to fulfillment. And the third one (Nazi Germany) was fulfilled right before the beast that looks like a bear (Russia) found its fulfillment. However, the part that does follow the chronology is the fourth wing of the leopard. That wing has not yet come. That wing is the Fourth Reich. Notice how each successive reich is more powerful and larger than the last. It is of the Fourth Reich that the words "given authority" apply. The European Union is its predecessor. It is a setup for the Fourth Reich.

When the European Union was established, it was meant to be a check on Germany by both France and the United Kingdom. However, since Germany has the strongest economy in the Euro (because of its manufacturing industry), and since the sovereign debt crisis hit Europe, Germany has become the dominant force in the EU. At some point in the near future there will be a charismatic leader who rises up in Germany; that will be the fourth head of the leopard beast. And when the crisis has become full blown, total authority will be handed over to Germany to deal with the crisis.

The threat of Russian aggression is another possible cause for handing over authority. Nations of the EU cannot defend against Russian invasion separately, but a centrally powerful EU could. Eastern Europe would especially be inclined to give Germany authority as a safeguard against Russian invasion, because they remember the oppression of the Soviet Union.

There's one nation in the EU right now which will not stay in the EU. It is the only nation in the EU that has retained its own currency. I'm talking about the United Kingdom. How hard will it be for the UK to exit the EU? Not hard at all. Many members of Parliament are already of the mind that the UK should exit the

EU. And its a growing movement; they're called "Euro skeptics". But that can only be said of the UK, because only the UK has retained its own currency, and nothing substantial would have to change if the UK did decide to exit the EU. Why will the UK exit the EU? Because the UK is also one of the four beasts. The leopard beast may be given authority over Europe, but it is not given authority over another beast. That is precisely why Hitler could conquer practically all of Europe, but stopped dead in his tracks when he tried to conquer the United Kingdom and Russia.

IX

The Vatican

It is at this point that I bring you back to the prophecy concerning the church in Thyatira. The woman Jezebel is punished by God's wrath, because she would not repent of all her false doctrine and idolatry. So how does it happen? The punishment of Jezebel comes at the hand of the Fourth Reich. It is the fourth wing of the leopard beast that acts as an instrument of divine judgment. As Hitler and the Third Reich did to the Jews, the Fourth Reich will do similarly to the Vatican and those Catholics close to the Vatican.

Why do I think this? Well, for one thing, it is a prophecy concerning the Vatican that has not yet been fulfilled, meaning it must be fulfilled sometime in the future.

Secondly, there is reason to think that God is establishing Jerusalem as the capital of all Christendom. Rome tries to make the claim, and I'm sure some people think of Rome as the capital of Christendom. But if God wishes to establish Jerusalem as the focal point for the global Christian community (I'll say more about this later in the book), then it makes sense that He would simultaneously remove all competing claims, such as the Vatican's claim.

A third reason, which is more speculative, is St. Malachy's prophecy, or the Prophecy of the Popes. It is a series of prophecies concerning the popes, written in an enigmatic way, that was supposed to have come from St. Malachy, a 12th century archbishop. Of course not everyone believes it, but it is an interesting prophecy. Those who do believe it to be real find a connection between each one of the prophecies and each one of the popes since the prophecy was given. The interesting thing about it is, according to the prophecy, Pope Francis is the last pope. The prophecy calls him "Petrus Romanus" (I believe the name has something to do with the birth name of Francis of Assisi, who was the inspiration for Bergoglio's name choice).

Rome as the fourth beast

There is one more beast to be mentioned, but its nothing like the first three. The first three represent world powers in Europe - Britain, Russia and Germany. The fourth is a true resurrection of the Roman Empire. Daniel calls the fourth beast terrifying and very powerful, different from the first three. It had large iron teeth and it crushed and devoured its victims, trampling underfoot whatever was left. And it had ten horns. The fact that its teeth are of iron associate it with the Roman Empire. Remember, iron represents the Roman Empire in the statue in Daniel 2. The ten horns represent ten kings. This is the kingdom of the Antichrist. The final horn, which uproots three and takes their place, is the Antichrist himself.

The interpretation that the angel gives (Daniel 7:15-27) aligns perfectly with the prophecies concerning the Antichrist in Revelation, and make it obvious that this final kingdom is the kingdom of the Antichrist.

Its not very relevant to the purpose of this book, because I do not believe the fourth kingdom will come soon. The final fulfillment of the third kingdom, the leopard beast, hasn't happened yet. But notice one thing: the description of the first beast in Revelation (chapter 13). It resembles a leopard, has feet like those of a bear, and it has the mouth of a lion. So why is the beast in Revelation, which represents the kingdom of the Antichrist, given every resemblance of the first three beasts in Daniel 7? It must be because the kingdom of the Antichrist brings the first three kingdoms - Britain, Russia, Germany - together into one. And at the center, where the Antichrist will make his capital, is Rome.

Is it all a coincidence? Is it a coincidence that the common point for Daniel 2 and 7 is Rome? Is it a coincidence that the beast in Revelation has the characteristics of a lion, a bear and a leopard? Is it a coincidence that Rome happens to be fairly centrally located in Europe (even if its a bit south)? Are the teeth of iron and legs of iron coincidental? Ask yourself, what part of this interpretation doesn't fit? What part seems out of line with other prophecies? What part does not make sense? Take however much time you need to look over the prophecies, to study the details, and to think about it. There are further details which I haven't put in this book.

Concerning the Vatican, I shouldn't have to say much to convince you that Rome is not the place for Christian leadership. There is really nothing Christian about Rome at all. It was Rome that persecuted Christians. The Vatican boasts of being built on Peter's body (as if Jesus meant His church would literally be built on the corpse of Peter), in the city where Peter was murdered. Rome is the city on seven hills. The city that is figuratively called Babylon. The city where Satan has his throne. The capital of the kingdom of the Antichrist. Its clear that the iron teeth of the fourth beast is an allusion to Rome and the legs of iron. One thing should be obvious: *Rome is not a Christian capital, and Christians should not look to Rome for leadership.*

X

The church in Sardis

We have concluded the meanings of the first four churches, and Thyatira takes us to the Roman Catholic and Eastern Orthodox churches. Those two branches of Christendom were the only branches, until a pivotal point in church history. The Reformation introduced Protestantism to the Christian world. No longer was the Roman Catholic Church the sole dominant church in Europe. Why the split? A new spirit emerged at the time of the Reformation; no longer was every Christian in Europe of the church in Thyatira. The spirit of the church in Sardis was emerging; that spirit is the spirit of Protestantism.

Jesus says of this church, "you have a reputation of being alive." The reformers gained a reputation for being zealous and true to the Bible. You can find many stories of martyrdom in books like the Martyrs Mirror or John Foxe's Book of the Martyrs, where Protestants died for their faith. This, and reformers like Luther, are much celebrated in Protestant churches. However, Jesus tells them, "but you are dead." The spiritual fervor of the reformers and the Protestant churches that came out of them was not as alive and well as it seemed. Some during the Reformation used violence against those they considered heretics, even though Jesus forbids us from executing judgment like that. Some continued the false practice of infant baptism. Some persecuted other Protestant sects. Some reacted to the

Roman Catholic emphasis on works, going to the opposite extreme of over-emphasizing faith. And worst of all, they could not agree enough to form themselves into one church, allowing Protestantism to become synonymous with denominations.

Jesus calls out to them, "wake up!" This is speculative, but maybe these words are somehow prophetic of the Great Awakening. Consider the chronology of the prophecy. First He states that they have a reputation for being alive but are dead. Note the reputation that reformers have. Then He says, "wake up!" The Great Awakening happens not long after the Reformation, relatively speaking.

Next He says, "strengthen what remains and is about to die." If you look at Protestant churches today, across the board there is weakness. Their doctrine is being watered down to accommodate the culture. While churches compromise on issues like gay marriage, thinking it will win them points with the younger crowd, they are losing the younger generation. Many Protestant churches are literally old and dying. They are "about to die" in the spiritual sense more importantly, but also in the physical sense as well. So the Great Awakening, while it deserves the 'Great', did not last. That is generally the problem with revivals: they imbue people with a spiritual zeal, but only for a short time. If we as Christians do not spiritually slumber, we won't have reason to talk about revival.

But not all is bad with the church in Sardis. Jesus acknowledges that they do have a few who have not stained their clothes. You can find in Protestant churches those who have a regular habit of doing good works, as opposed to the broader church whose "deeds are not complete". Those who haven't stained their white garments do remember the necessity of being righteous and doing good works. They are good Samaritans, missionaries, prison visitors, street preachers (unlike preachers who only preach for a salary, or televangelists who con people into giving money). They reject the move to be more acceptable to the culture. We only need to be acceptable to God; Jesus has already told us that the world will reject us. Those who keep their garments clean are not afraid of what their peers will think; though they be hated by the world, they stand strong on the truth.

Before I move on, it may do some good to talk about the primary reason behind Sardis' weakness. Jesus says He has not found their deeds complete in the sight of God. This implies a lack of good deeds. If we wonder why that might be, we need only look at Protestant doctrine: the Five Solas. Most notably, Sola Gratia (by grace alone) and Sola Fide (by faith alone). I fault these doctrines not necessarily for what they are, or might be, depending on how someone interprets them, but for what they aren't. They are not specific. They imply a view of soteriology (the study of salvation) which is entirely inaccurate. And Protestants will often expound on them with teaching that is entirely inaccurate. You're saved by faith alone, no good works can get you into heaven, they say. But that is a total lie. I realize you, Dear Reader, may have grown up with a Protestant background. So this may seem controversial to you, but give me the chance to explain. You have to read the Bible to see what is actually true, without allowing any human voice in your ear (without allowing any teaching to taint or shape what you're reading).

Sola Fide is wrong because the Bible says that all men will be judged according to their works (Romans 2:6, Matthew 16:27,

Revelation 2:23, 22:12, Psalm 62:12, Proverbs 24:12). Protestants counter this by saying that it only applies to unbelievers. So those who don't believe in Jesus will be judged by their works, and since their works aren't perfect, because God demands perfection, they will be damned; whereas believers will be given a magical pass. But the Bible never says this. It never speaks of two different judgments. It never says that believers will be given a pass on judgment day. It simply says that all men will be judged according to their works. It applies to both unbeliever as well as believer. Both to those who know all the right Sunday-school answers, and those who have never been to Sunday-school. Don't worry, God is a righteous Judge. He sees everything. He takes everything into account. But faith is not a magic ticket to heaven, and there are no magic words that will get you in. The demons have faith; even more faith than Jesus' own disciples, when Jesus was roaming around Israel.

Then the counter is, but its not "true" faith. Only true faith guarantees a spot in heaven; but again, upon the basis of faith and not works. How do we know true faith? Good works prove it. But don't try to do good works, because then you'll be putting your faith in works. You can be doing good works, but if its because you're not certain that your faith will save you, then your works are as filthy rags. I say, how then does good works prove true faith? If you need works to prove your faith, but you can't put faith in works, doesn't it leave you in a contradiction? Its impossible to make sense of Protestant soteriology. The whole thing is meant to defend Sola Fide, and Sola Fide is understood to mean that faith is your ticket to heaven. But it doesn't reconcile with some of the plain teachings in the Bible, which make it clear that you must do good works. So Protestant theologians try to reconcile it using complicated explanations, new words, distinctions and definitions; that is, mental gymnastics. I ask, can a child understand their explanations? If not, then there must be something wrong, because Jesus said the kingdom of God must be received as a little child receives something.

What then is the truth? How are we to make sense of soteriology? I think the easiest way to explain it is to go to Ephesians 2:8-10. Verses 8 and 9 are Protestant favorites. For by grace you have been saved, through faith, and not of works. See, we are saved by grace and faith, and works do nothing, right? Wrong. The Protestant tries to use this verse, and other similar verses, to make their case for Sola Fide. But if they mean that people will enter heaven on the basis of grace and faith, and not of works, then they are very much mistaken. Who is Paul speaking to? The Christian church in Ephesus. Are they in heaven? No. Does he say they are saved, or will be saved? He says that they have been saved. So this salvation has already taken place; clearly, he doesn't mean that these Ephesians have ascended into heaven. What does he mean? What could he possibly be talking about? Regeneration - being born again. He means that they have been born of the Holy Spirit by the grace of God, and that it happened through faith. Works did not facilitate their being born again. Baptism didn't cause it to happen. Circumcision didn't cause it. It was God's grace, which manifested itself through faith. Does it mean they don't have to do good works? Not at all! The very next verse reads, "created in Christ Jesus to do good works." Its no wonder then, the Bible tells us that every one will be judged according to their works. Its not a contradiction at all; for Paul was not talking about ascending into heaven on the basis of grace and faith, but rather being born again on the basis of grace and faith. Regeneration is what causes good works. The indwelling of the Holy Spirit causes the fruit of the Holy Spirit.

This is the reason Protestants lack in good works. Not only are good works not required in Protestant soteriology, but when you go about to do good works, it looks suspicious. It looks as though you put your faith in your own works, and anyone who grew up in a Protestant church knows that this is anathema. Hardly anything is more damning in a Protestant church than believing a "works gospel". So what you have is every encouragement to not do good works and every discouragement to do them. The obvious result is that Protestant churches are complacent and do little or nothing, which makes them sanctified country clubs essentially. You just have to go to church and have "true faith", spending the rest of your time trying to figure out what true faith looks like, and making sure you don't put faith in works. Or just conclude that religion is too complicated for you to understand and relegate it to Sunday mornings. Its no mystery that Sardis' works are not complete.

XI

The church in Philadelphia

We have now come to the church in Philadelphia. This church is the most relevant, because it is emerging in our own day. First we must understand what the open door represents; it is clearly figurative for something. An open door is an opportunity. So we would expect this open door to represent some great opportunity for the Christian church, particularly those who belong to the church in Philadelphia. I believe it is the internet. Just think, the internet is a portal to the outside world. Without leaving your house, you can communicate with hundreds or thousands of people all over the world. In the evangelical sense, this is wonderful.

Why would the open door be special for the church in Philadelphia? Jesus says that, though they have little strength, they have not denied His name and have kept His word. If a Christian is going to make good use of the internet to spread the truth, its important that he know the Bible and hold to it solidly. Heretics cannot make good use of the internet, because once they put their lies out there, they will be confronted and refuted. You see, the internet is sunlight. It is out in the "open". And in the open every claim is tested. The truth holds up, but lies are exposed as lies. For those who keep God's word, which is the truth, the internet is great. They have nothing to fear; they can roam around the internet like lions.

Jesus says the church in Philadelphia will be blessed. Those who are of the synagogue of Satan, who call themselves Jews but lie, will bow down and worship at the feet of the church in Philadelphia. This must be understood as a physical blessing. The church in Smyrna was blessed spiritually, but not physically, which is obvious because they were persecuted. But since those who are of the synagogue of Satan will bow down at the feet of the church in Philadelphia, there must be some visible reason. Jesus says, "they will acknowledge that I have loved you." If it is acknowledged that Jesus loves this church, especially by those who are of the synagogue of Satan, then the blessing bestowed upon this church is visible. Those who belong to the devil cannot recognize, and therefore cannot acknowledge, spiritual blessings. Although spiritual blessings are more important than physical blessings, because spiritual blessings are eternal and physical blessings are temporal, only physical blessings are seen, and thereby acknowledged, by those who do not belong to the Lord.

So what is the synagogue of Satan? The phrase appears both in this letter and in the letter to the church in Smyrna. In the letter to Smyrna it was literally the Jews. At that time, Jews would make all sorts of false accusations against Christians, and take every opportunity to blaspheme our Lord Jesus. Think about the words of Paul in Romans 2. Though they were Jews outwardly (they were circumcised in the flesh), they were not Jews inwardly, because they did not keep the commands of God (their hearts were not circumcised). This is why Jesus says they are not Jews. As for the synagogue of Satan in the letter to Philadelphia, it does not need to be the same as the one in Smyrna. Philadelphia relates to the present time, centuries after the letter was written.

Prophecies are often written using figurative language because the things they predict did not exist at the time it was written. For instance, "my servant David" is used to speak of the Messiah, whose name is not David but Jesus. God did not want to give away the name of the Messiah - Jesus - before it was time, so He used David's name to figuratively represent the Messiah. The same concept applies to prophecies of war in the modern era. Tanks, helicopters, jets and guns did not exist at the time that prophecies were written. There were not even Hebrew words for these things. For a prophet like Isaiah or Daniel, prophesying war in the modern era, to say "tank" or "helicopter" would have required them to make up a Hebrew word, and nobody at the time would have had a clue what they were talking about. Even translators wouldn't know what the word means, because it would only appear in that prophecy and nowhere else. So what would a prophet do? He would use words of things common at the time, like horses, chariots, bows and arrows, to figuratively represent tanks, helicopters, guns and rockets. The same applies with the synagogue of Satan, who call themselves Jews. What it represents, in the letter to Philadelphia, is the Muslim world. But since Islam did not exist at the time the prophecy was written (it would come over 500 years later), the prophecy could not say, "those who call themselves Muslims." So it says in a figurative sense, "those who call themselves Jews."

Muslims do call themselves Jews in a figurative sense. They do claim to be children of the promise given to Abraham, just through his son Ishmael rather than Isaac. If you want to read something funny, read the prophecy concerning Ishmael and compare it to Muslim Arab nations. There probably is some connection between Ishmael and Islam, but the promise given to Abraham was not given through Ishmael, it was given through

Isaac and the descendants of Isaac, Jesus being the primary one. So to understand what it means that the synagogue of Satan - the Muslim world - will bow down and worship at the feet of the church in Philadelphia, acknowledging that Jesus has loved them, we have to know a bit of the future. That's where other prophecies come into play.

But before we delve into all the other prophecies relating to our era, it would be good to look at the lessons that come out of this letter. There are two main points:

1. That its crucial to keep our views biblical. Philadelphia is commended for keeping Jesus' word. This can be taken to mean that it doesn't ignore or distort the Bible. It seeks for a true understanding of Scripture, and accepts what is plainly taught in Scripture.

2. Love. Philadelphia means 'city of brotherly love'. What this church does right is love. The essential manifestation of keeping Jesus' word is our love towards others, because God's word commands love more than anything else. The two greatest commandments are to love God will all heart, soul, mind and strength, and to love our neighbors as ourselves.

We as humans have the tendency to divide ourselves into groups. It may be ethnic groups, political groups, church denominations and religious sects, nationalities, gangs, clans, tribes, etc. Once we've decided that there's something to divide us, our tendency is to hate each other. Most wars happen because of one of these divisions and the hatred involved. If we want peace on earth, there has to be a solution to it. I tell you, the only solution is Christianity. Christianity teaches love. Not merely love for those who love us, or for those who are of our same party, nation, gang, clan or denomination; but love for our enemies as well. Christianity begs us to make peace with our enemies; as much as it is possible, to be at peace with everyone. It also asks us to put these divisions on the back shelf. We are Christians first; this should unite us. As for myself, I hate denominations. Its not that I hate the denominations themselves, but I hate the whole idea of even having denominations. I do not reject Christians who belong to denominations, or think they're any less Christian. But I do wish they would denounce the whole denominational system. We are Christians; why do we need to be anything else? Can't we be simply and only Christian?

Love will be crucial in the years ahead. There is so much suffering in the world. So much cruelty. So much pain. If families are to be healthy, and nations are to work properly, there has to be mutual love. There must be the things that accompany love. We must forgive and overlook offenses (how else could we have freedom of speech?). We must look after each other. The capitalist system works pretty good on a practical level, but its principles of self-reliance and survival of the fittest do nothing to protect the most vulnerable of society. Its not acceptable that we should let people fall through the cracks. We must take intelligent and moral steps to improve upon what we have, all in the name of love. Abortion must be ended. New mothers must be provided for. I'm not saying the answer is in government programs necessarily. But society itself, and particularly us Christians, must not ignore the need. Imagine a world that operates on the principle of love. We must infuse it into every part of our lives. Our words must radiate with love. Our actions should demonstrate love. A child should understand that his/her father's discipline is love. The child's parents should make it clear that discipline is love by explaining the reasons for it, and helping the child to mature from it. And making sure the discipline is balanced; not too mild and not too harsh. Our minor interactions with strangers should show love as well. Small things like holding a door open or saying "thank you". These might just brighten a person's day. I do believe love is the cure for depression. I could maybe write an endless treatise on the subject of love, but I'm sure you get the point. Love will revolutionize the world. It cannot be overstated how profound of an impact love will make, and what a wonderful result will come of it. That love will naturally come when we are filled with God's righteousness; that is, when we put our faith in Christ. We bring heaven down to earth when we truly and faithfully love each other.

XII

The war of Gog

We have to put the church in Philadelphia in the context of other prophecies, and other prophecies in the context of Philadelphia. Both the United States and Israel are related to the fulfillment of the promise to Philadelphia. I will show you how both are present in biblical prophecy. First let me take you to the book of Ezekiel, where the modern state of Israel was predicted thousands of years before it came to be.

Ezekiel 36 starts by prophesying to the land of Israel. It has become the possession of Israel's enemies. All the nations surrounding it have plundered it, and it has become desolate. But the prophecy says the land will produce fruit for His people, the nation of Israel. The people will be multiplied on the land, the towns and cities populated and the ruins rebuilt. One thing is clear from this prophecy in Ezekiel 36: it is predicting a time when the people of Israel will return to their homeland. The land was the possession of the enemy, but now it will be the possession of Israel. It was desolate when the enemy possessed it, but now it will be populated and fruitful when Israel possesses it. It says that Israel was scattered among the nations, driven out of their homeland by the judgment of God. But He will gather them together, bring them back to the land. Not for their sakes, but for the sake of His Holy Name.

Just think, has this not happened in the last century or so? The Jews were scattered among the nations, and Palestine was a barren wasteland. It was in the hands of Arabs, the historical enemies of Israel, until the Jews began to return to the land, and it became the official state of Israel. Now the land has prospered more than it ever has before. Israel is the most prosperous nation in the middle east. Read chapter 36 and think to yourself: what about this prophecy has not been fulfilled exactly as it says? Every word, every detail, is a prediction of the last hundred years. That is because chapters 36 through the end of the book deal with our day and age. They progress in chronological order. First, the people of Israel return to the land of Israel.

Yet it doesn't end there. There's one major event and turning point that must happen after Israel has returned to their homeland. Chapters 38 and 39 of Ezekiel describe a great war, or what would be a war if God didn't intervene. Gog leads a coalition of Arab nations against the new nation of Israel. We know these chapters are in chronological order, because the prophecy tells us in verse 8 they will go up against a land recovered from war, whose people have gathered from many nations to the land of Israel, which had long been desolate. So it basically repeats chapters 36 and 37 to put it in context. This coalition of Arab nations goes up against Israel with numbers "like a cloud covering the land". But on the mountains of Israel God will pour out His wrath and judgment on the enemies of Israel. There will be confusion, sword turned against sword, plague, hail and burning sulfur. Fire will rain down on the coasts of Gog, and the armies that went to invade Israel will be utterly destroyed. Why? The reason is to reveal Himself to the nations. To grasp the magnitude of it you need to read the passage itself.

He says, "in my zeal and fiery wrath I declare that at that time there shall be a great earthquake in the land of Israel. The fish of the sea, the birds of the air, the beasts of the field, every creature that moves along the ground, and all the people on the face of the earth will tremble at my presence. The mountains will be overturned, the cliffs will crumble and every wall will fall to the ground."

This is very serious. Israelis need to pay attention to this passage of Scripture. Not because their enemies will prevail, when their enemies mount an all-out assault, but because of this great earthquake. If the mountains are overturned, the cliffs crumble and every wall falls down, then this is a very serious earthquake. One that the people of Israel need to be ready for. If someone does not see it coming and take the necessary steps, like getting out of and away from every building, he will likely perish.

But maybe someone is thinking this is a stretch, that its too extraordinary to happen in our day. For one, I would point out that technology has made the news in any one part of the world instantly available to all other parts of the world for the first time in history. So when it says that all people will tremble at His presence, its reasonable to think all people will hear it, and even see it as its happening, and that that would cause people to tremble. Secondly, if its going to happen, its going to begin with an invasion of Arab nations. What is Gog? I believe Gog is Turkey. If I'm right, Turkey will lead a coalition of nations against the nation of Israel. The other possibility is that Gog represents Russia. I realize most interpretations see Gog as Russia, but I do believe Turkey is a more likely candidate. If either one of these nations leads a coalition of Arab nations against Israel, you know what else is about to happen. All you need to do is read the prophecy in Ezekiel 38 and 39 and connect the dots. If anyone is skeptical, there's no need to believe what I'm saying, until you see the fulfillment of the prophecy begin to unfold. Then there will be desperate need to pay attention, and prepare for the greatest earthquake the world will ever see.

So when will the war of Gog in Ezekiel 38 and 39 happen? I believe it will happen in the year 2018, and there's three reasons for that:

1. It must happen pretty soon. If the war of Gog follows the return of the Jews to the land of Israel, then the war of Gog is coming soon, because the Jews have already returned to the land of Israel.

2. I believe there is a hint in the book of Daniel. Its in the seventy sevens prophecy in Daniel 9. "Know and understand this: from the issuing of the decree to restore and rebuild Jerusalem until the Anointed One (Christ), the ruler, comes, there will be seven 'sevens,' and sixty-two 'sevens'." In all there are 70 sevens, which is stated in verse 24. The final seven, as most people interpret it, is the tribulation period. Many interpret the other sevens as predicting the first coming of Christ, but I believe its actually a prediction of His second coming. For one reason, because there was never actually a decree to rebuild Jerusalem before Jesus' first coming. There was a decree to rebuild the wall of Jerusalem, and a decree to rebuild the temple in Jerusalem, but never a decree to rebuild Jerusalem itself. Secondly, the Antichrist is obviously present in verse 27, if not verse 26 as well. When Jesus talks about the end times in Matthew 24, He quotes verse 27 of Daniel 9 in Matthew 24:15. Since it wasn't fulfilled with Jesus' first coming, and pertains to His second coming, can we know when the decree happened?

Has it happened? The decree to rebuild and restore Jerusalem did indeed happen; it happened in the 20th century. Just two years after Israel reclaimed Jerusalem in the Six Days War (1967) the Knesset passed a resolution (in 1969) forming the Company for the Reconstruction and Development of the Jewish Quarter. There you have a decree to actually rebuild Jerusalem itself, and it happened just decades ago. That makes 1969 our starting point. From there, if every seven represents a Sabbath Year (seven years), there's 490 years until Jesus returns: 1,969 + 490 = 2,459. There you have the year of Christ's return.

I'm sure some people are thinking, "but wait, didn't Jesus say that no one knows the day or hour of His return?" That is correct. Jesus said, "no one knows the day or hour." Notice that He specifically said day or hour. If He meant, "the time of My return," He could have said "time". If He meant that no one would know the year of His return, He could have said, "the day, the hour or the year." But He didn't say year, and He didn't give a vague reference to the time of His return; He specifically said day or hour, leaving the possibility open for someone knowing the year.

But none of that applies to the war of Gog. The interesting thing about this prophecy is that its not simply 70 sevens. It is divided up: 7 sevens, 62 sevens and one final seven. The final seven must be the tribulation period, but we have no idea what the 7 sevens are, or why he doesn't just say 69 sevens. And Daniel, or the angel speaking to Daniel, does not give us the reason. Let's do the math: 7 sevens is 49 years. If we start at 1969 and go forward 49 years, we end up at the year 2018. Since the year 2018 is soon, and the war of Gog should happen soon, and this prophecy in Daniel 9 seems to be hinting at something significant in the year 2018, maybe the war of Gog will happen in 2018.

3. The third reason for the year 2018 is the founding of the state of Israel, which happened in the year 1948. From 1948 to 2018, do the math: its 70 years. 2018 is the seventieth anniversary of the state of Israel. Why does this matter? Because we've seen God use a 70 year time period before. The Israelites were first exiled for 70 years. As I've heard it, it was one year for every Sabbath Year they neglected to honor (70 Sabbath Years = 490 years of rebellion). If the year 2018 is both the 49th year after the decree to rebuild and restore Jerusalem, and the 70th year after the founding of the state of Israel, its an odd coincidence, isn't it? I do not believe its a coincidence, but that it signifies the event of the war of Gog.

What is the significance of the war of Gog? What does it accomplish? The war of Gog is a major turning point, not just for the nation of Israel, but for the whole world as well. God reveals Himself to many nations, as the prophecy says. Proof of God's existence already exists, but you must search for it. In this miraculous act, through which God saves the nation of Israel, proof of God's existence will be right there in front of everyone. Anyone who would claim to be an atheist at that point should be put in an insane asylum. As it is now, one might be able to ignore the evidence and proof of the Bible's veracity, since it requires some research and meditation to discover. Dull minds will always miss what isn't obvious; that is, right in front of them and plain. But when the war of Gog comes to a conclusion, the fact of God's existence, and that He is the God of Israel, will be right in front of everyone and plain. Expect to see people converting to the religion of our Lord. How quickly, I'm not sure.

But it will certainly be a turning point for the world. In addition, it will be the major turning point in Israel's history.

Israel is prophesied to accept Jesus as their Messiah in more than one place in the Bible. In Zechariah it prophesies that the nation of Israel will mourn for the one they have pierced (Zechariah 12:10). Who did Israel pierce? It says that on that day the mourning in Jerusalem will be great. What day is that? I believe it happens at the conclusion of the war of Gog, that this is the time in which the nation of Israel is grafted back into the kingdom of God, as Paul speaks of in Romans 11. They realize they were wrong for rejecting Jesus all these years. See what God says in Ezekiel 39:22-23: "From that day forward the house of Israel will know that I am the LORD their God. And the nations will know that the people of Israel went into exile for their sin, because they were unfaithful to me. So I hid my face from them and handed them over to their enemies, and they all fell by the sword." The Holocaust is still fresh in the mind of every Jew. The day Jews realize the underlying cause of the Holocaust - that God had handed them over to their enemies because of their sin and rejection of Jesus - will be a hard day for them. Do you see why the weeping in Jerusalem will be great? Not only because they were killed in the Holocaust and many pogroms, but also because the wrath of God is still on them. Yes, they were saved from their enemies in this war. Not for their sakes, God says, but for the sake of the name and fame of Almighty God. But even when the nation of Israel is saved from total annihilation, a great earthquake hits the land of Israel unlike any before. Of course a number of people are killed in the earthquake; another reason the mourning in Jerusalem will be great. Those who recognize the fulfillment of the prophecy as its happening, and take the necessary precaution, will be saved from the earthquake. As you can imagine, this is a time that shakes the nation of Israel to the core. Everything for them is changed. You'll understand why this is as we go deeper into the meaning of the prophecies. God has a plan for the world, and Israel is at the center of it.

XIII

The white horseman

Next we must understand the meaning of the white horseman, and how the United States relates to both Philadelphia and Israel, and what the prophecies declare. We have discovered that there are nations in the world today represented as different beasts in the Bible. We talked about the beasts in Daniel 7, how the lion beast is Great Britain, the beast that looks like a bear Russia, and the leopard beast Germany. If these nations are present in the Bible, one would think that a nation such as the United States, which is not the least bit inferior as far as size and significance to the others, might also be present in the Bible.

There are four horsemen in Revelation 6. The first is a white horseman, the second is a red horseman, the third a black horseman, and the fourth is pale. What you often see, as interpretations of this prophecy, is something about Christ or something about the Antichrist. Popular interpretation of prophecy erroneously sees only two characters: Christ and the Antichrist. So the two main interpretations of the white horseman are that its Christ or the Antichrist; but both are wrong. It cannot be Christ, because Christ is the white horseman in Revelation 19, and believe me, the two cannot be compared. The greatness of the white horseman in Revelation 19 far exceeds the one in Revelation 6. It cannot be the Antichrist, because the color white always represents righteousness in the book of Revelation, and the Antichrist is the opposite of righteous. Some say its because he presents himself as righteous. But it doesn't make any sense. Would God cater to the propaganda of the Antichrist? Does God care how the Antichrist presents himself, as opposed to reality? What we see in Revelation is a prophecy of reality - what things really are or will be - not a reflection of the false propaganda of the enemy. Besides, the Antichrist is already represented in Revelation as a beast, and in Daniel as a beast. It makes more sense to believe that the white horseman is something entirely different: a third character. Once we get out of the rut of thinking there are only two characters in biblical prophecy, it becomes easy to interpret these four horseman. In fact, what they represent becomes rather obvious.

The white horseman is the United States of America. I know this from a number of hints and signs. You'll want to pay close attention to this, especially if you're an American. The first horseman comes from the opening of the first seal. So maybe there is a seal that will give us a clue as to what the first horseman is? If the white horseman is the United States of America, what seal could it be? The Great Seal of the United States. On the back of the one dollar bill you can see both the reverse and obverse of the Great Seal.

On the obverse (front) you see a bald eagle, representing the United States. In its right talon it has an olive branch, with thirteen leaves and thirteen olives, representing the original thirteen states (I'm a Virginian, so the founding of our nation, and our nation's founders, are especially close to home for me). In its left talon there are thirteen arrows. The white horseman, the prophecy says, has a bow. A bow does no good without arrows, so there we have one clue. But the other distinguishing mark of the white horseman is the crown he is given. These two things, the bow and the crown, are the two key features of the white horseman. Nothing immediately jumps out, as far as the olive branch and the crown the horseman is given. But dig a little deeper and we discover another clue in the olive branch. In the Greek that Revelation was written in, there are two words that mean crown. One is stephanos, the victor's crown. The other is diadema, the royal crown. The many crowns on Jesus'

head in Revelation 19:12 are diadema. The crown that is given to the white horseman in Revelation 6 is stephanos (another reason for thinking the white horseman in chapter 6 is not the same as Jesus, the white horseman in chapter 19). The victor's crown comes from the ancient Greek Olympics. Today we give a gold medal to the victor, but in the original Olympics it was a wreath that was given to the victor. I'm sure you've seen it before, the semicircle crown wreath; Roman emperors would wear a similitude of it. And the kind of wreath given for first place? A wreath made out of an olive branch. That is the victor's crown. That is the crown given to the white horseman.

Already we have two clues on the Great Seal, the arrows correlating with the bow, and the olive branch correlating with the crown. But what do these symbolize in reality? There has to be more than just a couple clues; there has to be an actual fulfillment of these objects in the history of the United States. A bow represents long range weaponry. It was right around the time of WWII, and especially at the end of it, that the United States developed its long range weaponry. I'm talking about bombers, missiles, ICBMs, and especially nuclear bombs. During the Cold War we further developed our long range weaponry. What would the modern fulfillment of an arrow be? A missile, a rocket, an ICBM, etc. And a bow? The stealth B2 bomber even looks a bit like a bow; not that that's the reason for associating the B2 with a bow in prophecy, but the B2 bomber does function as a modern fulfillment of a figurative bow. It just happens to have a similar shape as well. The United States has far more long range weaponry than any other nation on earth.

Then the white horseman is given a crown. What does the crown and the olive branch stand for? Since it is the victor's crown, there has to be some victory the United States won. And not just any kind of victory; the crown was given to the victor of the foot race in the ancient Olympics. It has to be a race the United States won. No, I'm not talking about the arms race. I'm talking about something more important than that: the space race. We won the space race by putting a man on the moon. And if that doesn't seem remarkable to you, just note the fact that the United States is the first to put a man on the moon, and the only to put a man on the moon. Over forty years after it happened, still no other nation on earth has done it. It was Apollo 11 that put a man on the moon for the first time, winning the space race for America. And if you're not convinced that it was the fulfillment of the crown given to the white horseman, just take a look at the mission insignia for Apollo 11:

You can see it on the back of a silver dollar, if you have one. Yes, all of the clues are right there waiting to be discovered. I will point out another briefly: the "bald" eagle got its name from the English word piebald; we just shortened it, because "bald eagle" has a better ring to it than "piebald eagle". The word piebald means a white spot, or sometimes 'crowned with white'. Another correlation between the white horseman and the US, as represented by the white spotted eagle. The United States is the first horseman of the Apocalypse. The first seal of the Apocalypse has been opened, and you've seen it many thousands of times if you use American currency.

Yet there's one more clue. Its found in Zechariah 6. There are four chariots with different colored horses, which are the four spirits of heaven. They go out from the presence of the Lord; the one with black horses goes to the north, the one with white horses goes to the west, and the one with dappled horses goes to the south. Leaving the one with red horses to go east. But to understand where they actually go, we have to know the starting point. What is the presence of the Lord? If we were to put it anywhere on the map, it would have to be the temple located in Jerusalem. And Jerusalem just happens to be in the center of the earth. Of course the earth is round, so no point on the earth's surface is literally the center. But when we make world maps, or when we commonly talk about the world's regions, Asia is to the east, the Americas are to the west, and Jerusalem is right at the center. The Pacific Ocean, being as big as it is, is a convenient place to make the cut; so that's where the International Date Line is. Interesting thing about this prophecy is that the colors of the horses (not to mention the number) are the exact same as the horsemen in Revelation 6. In the word of God, instances like that are not coincidental. With Jerusalem as the starting point, the chariots with black horses end up in Europe, the red end up in east Asia, the pale or dappled (the color is the same, although the word in Zechariah is Hebrew, and the word in Revelation is Greek, which explains the difference in translations) end up in Africa, and the white end up in the western hemisphere, specifically in the United States, if you follow Jerusalem's latitude westward. That gives us another clue as to where each of these four horsemen originate. As for the red horseman with a big sword, which takes peace from the earth, it must be China. The black horseman represents famine, and the pale horseman represents plague. They come much closer to the end times, and being themselves a catalyst for the rise of the Antichrist.

Revelation says the white horseman rides out as a conqueror bent on conquest. The result of this conquest is implied in the prophecy concerning the red horseman. Yes, the red horseman is given a big sword and makes war, but it doesn't specifically say "makes war". Instead it says "takes peace from the earth". This tells us that the red horseman makes war, but in addition, that there was peace on earth to be taken. A nation can make war in the context of war, but a nation cannot "take peace from the earth" where there is no peace to be taken. And that implies that the previous horseman, the white horseman, creates peace with its conquest.

Probably the greatest example in history of conquest resulting in peace is the Pax Romana. And if the Pax Romana was the result of Rome conquering the entire Mediterranean Sea, then any peace resulting from America's conquest will come only after the US has conquered the world. As the Mediterranean Sea was then, so the world is now. The level of technology they had then connected the peoples of the Mediterranean to make it their world. But the level of technology we have today makes the world an increasingly small place. There is reason to think the world will inevitably be conquered by one world power. I don't mean the reason is prophetic, although prophecy confirms it. I mean there is a natural dynamic at work, in which the strongest power will inevitably conquer all other powers and suppress their ability to fight back. It was that dynamic at work in the Mediterranean when the Romans conquered it. The same dynamic shows itself in the way the world is setup today. If the US doesn't conquer the world, some other world power will.

I believe the prophecy concerning the white horseman, which is concerning the USA, has not been entirely fulfilled yet. That America has yet to do much of its conquest. It is impossible for the red horseman, China, to take peace from the earth today, since peace has not been established on earth today. Furthermore, we cannot say the degree to which the US has already conquered matches a biblical proportion. Prophecy does not talk about a nation bent on conquest, if its just a little bit of conquest. I have more reason for thinking the fulfillment of this prophecy is yet to come, as you'll see in the following chapters.

XIV

A new world order

To understand the bigger picture, or what God has planned for the world in the years to come, we must understand the meaning on the reverse of the Great Seal as well. When God draws our attention to the Seal by what is on front, its not merely to look at the front, but to notice a few things on the back as well. The back will put American conquest into context. It all fits together - American conquest, a new Israeli nation, an emerging church in Philadelphia.

On the back of the Great Seal is an unfinished pyramid. The pyramid represents both the nation and the Constitution. This is evident in the Roman numerals at the base of the pyramid, which amount to 1776, the Declaration of Independence, and the Latin, "Novus Ordo Seclorum". The Declaration of Independence was when the nation was born, and the Constitution is the Novus Ordo Seclorum (New World Order). The Constitution is the final result of what began in 1776. Because pyramids are begun at the bottom, the Roman numerals are at the bottom. And because our Constitution is a world order, it is the New World Order spoken of in Latin.

But you'll notice that the pyramid is unfinished. There's two ways of looking at that. The Eye of Providence (or the "All-seeing Eye") stands directly above the unfinished pyramid. It could mean that the New World Order is completed by God Himself, or it could mean that there will be further additions in the future. And it could mean both. There may be more reason for an amendment process to the Constitution than you thought. Not just the reason that its imperfect and therefore subject to change, but also the reason that it was destined to be added to, even in our future.

The New World Order will ultimately look like this: God will be King over Israel, Israel will have authority over the United States of America, and the US will have conquered the world. In effect, Israel will lead the world - righteously - with the United States enforcing its rule. There is a bond between Israel and the US which goes beyond any sort of alliance. It is more than just an alliance, and its a bond that will only get stronger in the future. If you want to see evidence of this, look again at the obverse of the Great Seal. God puts hints in plain sight, for when the designer put thirteen stars above the eagle's head, he did not arrange them in any random way. What is the Star of David doing above the eagle? Just as the Eye of Providence over the pyramid symbolizes the US as "one nation under God", so too the Star of David above the eagle has symbolism. We are one nation under God, and we are one nation under Israel. And Israel is one nation under God, or at least will be in the near future.

Don't let this affect your pride, Dear American, because it doesn't limit the freedom or honor of being an American. It is the will of God, and the will of God cannot be thwarted. The will of God is good as well, and you will see just how good the New World Order will be, once you're able to see it and compare it to today. There is no problem submitting to the will of Israel, when the will of Israel is submitted to God. Likewise, the world will see no problem submitting to the will of the US, when the will of the US is submitted to the will of Israel, and the will of Israel is submitted to the will of God. All will be submitted to God, either directly or indirectly. That is the New World Order. Today it stands as an unfinished pyramid, but God will finish it. This is why, as I've said before, God has a plan, and Israel is at the center of it. This is why it is important that Israel be reborn spiritually. This is why the nation of Israel must accept Jesus as Messiah. This is why the weeping in Jerusalem must be great. God prepares a people like Israel, who He plans to set at the forefront of nations, with chastisement. Such a great responsibility - to lead all the nations of the earth - must be taken very seriously, and it must be held by a nation that is humbly submitted to the will of God. Thus God has not left the nation of Israel untouched, but has punished them and purged them, causing them (in time) to cry and weep bitterly over their years of rejecting Him. This sets the nation with the right mind, the right attitude and spirit, to take on such a responsibility. A nation of priests, the Bible says.

Not only will Israel be at the center of the world, but Jerusalem will be at the center of the world. Remember how Rome is about to be judged for her sins? That woman Jezebel in Revelation 2, which is the Vatican, is about to be punished for her idolatry, and it will come at the hands of the Fourth Reich. One of the reasons it will happen soon is to make way for Jerusalem. Rome claims to be the capital of all Christendom, and some believe it. But in the future Jerusalem actually will be the capital of all Christendom. God Himself will establish it. And to eliminate any doubt, He will remove Rome's false claim to being Christendom's capital. There cannot be two; there must only be one.

How will it be known that Jerusalem is the capital of all Christendom? By the building of a third temple. John prophesies that the Antichrist, when he comes, will desecrate a wing of the temple by putting an abomination there. If he is going to desecrate the temple, there has to be a temple. Notice, John wrote those words in the 90s (not the 1990s, just the 90s). The second temple was destroyed in 70 AD, which means there was no temple at the time John wrote Revelation. Furthermore, Jesus reinforces the prophecy given in Daniel when He talks about an abomination that causes desolation in the holy place, and says, "let the reader understand." There's no way to interpret this as applying to the second temple, because there never was an abomination that caused desolation between the time Jesus said it and 70 AD, when the temple was destroyed. It must apply to a third temple.

Indeed, there will be a third temple. Why haven't they built one yet? The reason they haven't built a third temple yet, in spite of the fact that many Jews would love to build a new temple, is the Dome of the Rock. The Dome of the Rock stands on the Temple Mount, the only place a true temple of God can be built. To tear it down would cause a massive riot in the Muslim world. Muslims already hate Israel (the reason Turkey will be able to form a coalition to attack Israel), but to tear down the Dome of the Rock would be just the excuse they need. And the leadership in Israel is not about to give their Muslim neighbors an excuse to go to war. The peace in the middle east is a very fragile and tense peace. The Knesset would never approve a measure to tear down the Dome of the Rock.

Then how can a third temple be built? The answer is obvious; its already been shown in this book. When the war of Gog happens, as Ezekiel says, there will be a massive earthquake. It says that every wall will collapse. Certainly this includes the Dome of the Rock. Besides, it wouldn't be right for Israel to build a third temple before the war of Gog, before the mourning in Jerusalem, before their conversion to Christianity. Only after all of that happens, when Jews have become united with Christians by one faith in Christ, does it make sense that a third temple would be built; a symbol of unity of faith, and a symbol of the New World Order.

The union between Christian and Jew is prophesied in Ezekiel 37, when it talks about the stick of Joseph and the stick of Judah. The stick of Joseph represents the Christian Church, and the stick of Judah represents the Jews. For the first time in history Jews and Christians will be completely united in one faith, which has already begun to happen, since more Christians embrace Israel, and more Jews are becoming messianic. A third temple, to symbolize and celebrate this union, just seems right. A physical object that says, "here is the symbolic center of God's kingdom on earth." Something to signify the capital of all Christendom. A necessary result of prophecy, a manifestation of God's will, and the ultimate success of Christian Zionism.

All of this is the fulfillment of the promise to the church in Philadelphia. The New World Order represents a new day in the history of man; a new era will dawn. Why does the synagogue of Satan worship at the feet of the church in Philadelphia? You see, when the war of Gog happens, and God pours out His wrath on the enemies of Israel, every Muslim on earth will know the true God is the God of Israel, and Israel will know that Jesus is the Christ. As it is now, Muslims persecute Christians in many parts of the world. Places like Pakistan, Syria, Nigeria, Indonesia, Sudan, Ethiopia, Egypt, Iraq and Iran have seen a massive increase in Muslim persecution against Christians. Pakistan has a blasphemy law that puts Christians in prison, even when the accusations may not be true. And if a Christian is released by the justice system, there's a good chance he will fall victim to a lynch mob. In Syria, since the civil war began, hundreds of Christians in Sadad were massacred by Islamists, and many hundreds elsewhere. Christians have no sense of security because of Islamists and the general chaos of war, and many of their churches have been burned. Similarly, the Coptic Christians in Egypt have faced persecution since Mubarak was ousted and the civil war begun. In northern Nigeria thousands have been killed by the Islamist gang Boko Haram. These are just a few examples. Churches burned down, anti-Christian laws passed, mobs attacking Christians, pastors imprisoned for preaching the gospel. But all of that will change when the war of Gog happens.

The promise to the church in Philadelphia, that those of the synagogue of Satan will worship at their feet, will be kept when God reveals Himself to the nations. Israel will be set at the head of all nations, and the US will go out and conquer to enforce a new set of rules. It is then that Muslims will have to acknowledge that Christ has loved our Christian brothers and sisters. They will be powerless to persecute Christians any longer. The purpose of the US conquering the world will be to put an end to persecution. Christians who have suffered the most will be shown the highest preferential treatment. They will go from prisons to palaces. They will be offered the highest positions of authority in every nation, because they have proven their faithfulness to Christ. It is then that (former) Muslims, who once persecuted Christians, will know that Jesus loves the church in Philadelphia; and they will be forced to acknowledge it.

You see how each prophecy is connected? How the fulfillment of the one is dependent on the fulfillment of the other? There cannot be a third temple, unless the Dome of the Rock is demolished. The earthquake during the war of Gog will demolish the Dome of the Rock. The church in Philadelphia cannot be physically blessed, unless the situation of persecution against Christians is changed. Because of the conquest of the white horseman, the situation will be changed.

XV

The harbinger

But maybe you are wondering, if white represents righteousness, how can the United States be the white horseman? We are hardly righteous. We are a nation going further into immorality and sin everyday; if white represents righteousness, it couldn't be the US. All of this is true. That's why the United States must experience a sort of purgatory, just like Israel. In a New World Order, both the US and Israel will be given incredible power and incredible responsibility. As we've discovered already, the war of Gog is a humbling time for the nation of Israel, in order to prepare it for that responsibility. Could there be a humbling for the US as well? If we are to be a shining city on a hill, which we certainly are not now, there must be some pivotal moment. There must come a judgment for America's sins, and a reminder for all future generations that God is supreme, and that His word must not be violated. We here in America have violated His word, and we will have to pay the price.

There is a book called the Harbinger, written by Jonathan Cahn. In it he points out 9 parallels between the details of 9/11 and a prophecy in Isaiah 9:10 that he calls harbingers (warning signs). I'll just highlight a few of them here, since you can buy his book to see the rest of the story. There are many uncanny similarities between the prophecy in Isaiah 9:10 and the events surrounding

9/11. I promise you, it is worth your time to read it and discover them.

The most uncanny is maybe the official congressional response to 9/11, given by Senate majority leader Tom Daschle on 9/12. Towards the end of the speech he quotes the verse in Isaiah 9:10: "The bricks have fallen, but we will rebuild with dressed stone. The sycamores have been felled, but we will plant cedars in their place." Its really odd that he would quote this verse, as if its something we as a nation should be saying in response to 9/11. In the context of the passage in Isaiah 9, this verse is the northern kingdom's arrogant response to a warning given from God. God allowed the Assyrians to attack the coastal towns of the kingdom, showing the Israelites that their hedge of protection was down. Instead of repenting and turning to God, the Israelites had a defiant and arrogant attitude. And we have shown the same kind of defiance in response to 9/11. Rather than turning to God as we should have, we have turned further away. The moral condition of America has gotten worse since 9/11.

Another harbinger is the dressed stone. In the place where the bricks had fallen - Ground Zero - they placed a massive memorial stone. A carved stone, just as the prophecy says. For another, near Ground Zero, between it and St. Paul's Chapel, there was a sycamore tree that took the brunt of the force when the towers collapsed. It saved the chapel, but the tree was uprooted and knocked over. It became known as the Tree of Hope. In its place they planted a coniferous tree. According to Jonathan, the Hebrew word that is translated as "cedar" can refer to any coniferous tree. These are just a few examples; I won't try to point out every detail of the book. To sum it up, there are a number of uncanny details that correlate to just one verse of the Bible. What does it mean? A warning.

The second part of Jonathan's book is like the sequel to 9/11 and the 9 harbingers. He points out that when Israel did not keep the Sabbath Year commandment, it became a year of judgment. Every seven years Israel would be met with some form of judgment for disobeying God's commands. He draws a parallel between that and the economic collapse of 2008. The economic collapse happened seven years after 9/11. And the two largest Dow Jones Index declines of the last decade, which both set records, occurred exactly seven years apart, to the day, by the Hebrew calendar. It was September 17, 2001, which is the 29th of Elul on the Hebrew calendar, and September 29, 2008, which is also the 29th of Elul. Jonathan follows this pattern forward, to the year 2015, and says there will be a stock market crash on September 13th of that year. But I question his judgment on this final point: September 13, 2015 is a Sunday. I believe there is more to the story.

There is one thing missing in Jonathan's book. He says the nine harbingers are a warning. He says there will be another economic collapse. But do the nine harbingers really mean the US will have an economic collapse every seven years? Is that really the fulfillment of the warning? After all, when the northern kingdom of Israel disregarded the warning God gave them, it was far worse than an economic crisis. The whole nation went into exile. The real question remains: the nine harbingers are a warning for what exactly? Its a question Jonathan doesn't answer in his book. So I went to the passage in Isaiah where the prophecy is found. God must be calling our attention to this passage; there must be something there for Americans to notice. Indeed there is.

A few verses after Isaiah 9:10 it says, "therefore the LORD will cut off head and tail from Israel, palm branch and bulrush in one day. The elder and the honorable, he is the head; the prophet who teaches lies, he is the tail." The interesting thing about this verse is that it was never fulfilled. Even if you take the words "one day" to mean a short period of time, it would still not be fulfilled with the invasion of the northern kingdom. The invasion and deportation of the northern kingdom took place over a span of about twenty years. The final city to be captured was Samaria, and it was besieged for three years. If you think as I do regarding Scripture, you know every verse has its purpose, and every prophecy finds its fulfillment somewhere. So if these two verses in Isaiah were not fulfilled in the northern kingdom of Israel, and God is calling our attention to this passage by the harbingers surrounding 9/11, maybe these couple verses apply to the United States. If so, it would be a dual prophecy: a prophecy given concerning two different events at different times in history (The prophecy Jesus gives in Matthew 24 is an example of this; it concerns both the destruction of Jerusalem in 70 AD and the end times Armageddon).

If it does apply to the United States, we would have to understand what is meant by head and tail, the elder and honorable, and the prophet who teaches lies. The elder and honorable apply to the leadership of the nation. That leadership is in DC, as the political capital, but also in New York City, as the financial capital of the nation. The corporate leaders in America have as much power as political leaders in America, which is evidenced by how much sway lobbyists have over legislators. So if the head - the leadership - is the elder and the honorable, maybe that represents two entities instead of one. And if the head represents two cities - DC and NYC - maybe the tail also represents a city. If there is any city in America that would be "the prophet who teaches lies", what city would that be? What city dominates the television? That would be Los Angeles and Hollywood. These three cities represent three capitals in America. Washington DC is the political capital. New York City is the financial capital. Los Angeles is the entertainment capital. Just think, what cities were targeted on 9/11? If 9/11 is a harbinger of something bad to come, and God is going to cut off head and tail in one day (just like 9/11 happened in one day), it stands to reason the fulfillment of this prophecy may be in another attack. This time, however, instead of a few buildings being destroyed, entire cities will be destroyed. How would entire cities be destroyed? By a nuclear attack.

Maybe you think I'm crazy. It would be easy to dismiss this as just a theory of some nut. And maybe it is far-fetched. But there are a few things we know:

1. The harbingers must be warning us of some event.

2. God is calling our attention to this passage of Scripture in Isaiah 9.

3. Isaiah 9:14-15 did not find its fulfillment in the northern kingdom of Israel.

There's one more piece of the puzzle that just might convince you. Remember 70 years in exile? Seven multiplied by ten, both numbers signifying completion. Remember how it is 70 years from Israel's founding to the 49th year after the decree to rebuild and restore Jerusalem? If a nuclear attack on US soil in 2015 represents a turning point for America, let's try the 70 year rule. Let's start in 2015, which is the next 7th year, and the 14th year after 9/11, and go back 70 years. We end up in 1945. What was significant about that year? The end of WWII. And when did the war end? Officially, in September. It was on August the 6th and 9th that we dropped nuclear bombs on Hiroshima and Nagasaki. On August the 15th the emperor of Japan decided to surrender. That surrender took place in Tokyo harbor aboard the USS Missouri on September the 2nd. That is why President Truman declared September the 2nd to be VJ day (Victory over Japan Day).

The attack on 9/11 happened on the 23rd of Elul, according to the Hebrew calendar. Let us suppose that the Hebrew calendar should be our means of dating this, since the prophecy itself was written in Hebrew. The 23rd of Elul in the year 1945 was September the 1st. Of course the 1st is not the 2nd. But take this date - September 1, 1945 - and do a Google search, see what you find. You find the announcement given by Truman of the official surrender of the Japanese. That's odd. How does Truman announce the surrender a day before it happens? Its because the surrender took place at 9:30 am in Tokyo Harbor. 9:30 am in Japan is 8:30 pm east coast time, of the previous day. So while it was September the 2nd in Japan, it was the 1st in America. And September 1, 1945 was the 23rd of Elul in the year 5705, according to the Hebrew calendar. The attack on 9/11 happened on the 56th anniversary of the surrender of Japan and the end of WWII, if we go by the Hebrew calendar. And the 23rd of Elul on the next seventh, in 2015, will be the 70th anniversary of the surrender of Japan. Does it make sense that 70 years after we dropped nuclear bombs on Japan, that nuclear bombs would be used against us? Does it make sense that it would be on the exact same day as the surrender of Japan? Well, 9/11 happened on the exact same day. That day, in 2015, is September the 7th.

The purpose of me writing this book is to warn people of these coming events. Especially those who live in these cities. My message to them: move. Get out of the city. If you think I'm just a crazy guy with crazy ideas, that's fine. But at least, with the small chance that I might be right, find some reason to leave the city on the week of September the 7th, 2015. A vacation, get away, or something. Why not? September the 7th of that year just so happens to be Labor Day. Take a day off and go visit your family in the country. Just make sure to leave the night before. If you know someone living in one of these cities, warn them. Either tell them what I'm telling you, or give them this book. There's no way to stop the fulfillment of prophecy. No government agency is going to take something like this seriously. If they did, they would prevent it from happening. But since they won't take it seriously, its possible. What can you do about it? Just tell people to leave these cities, or get yourself out if need be. Like Lot leaving the city of Sodom; the city itself cannot be saved, but the people inside the city may be saved, if they listen to the voice of an angel (the word angel simply means messenger from God).

XVI

The night

What we see today is the night before the dawn. It is the darkest part of the night. The darkness has slowly grown darker. And before the Sun dawns upon our land, the darkness of our land will result in judgment and death. Over 50 million preborn babies have been murdered in the US since Roe v. Wade. That's over 1 million legally sanctioned murders each year for the last 40 years. If Hitler deserves hell for having 7 million killed, what does the US deserve for having 50 million killed? What should be the result of God's anger? Or how about the fact that we daily affront Him and His word, saying homosexuality is not a sin, that its natural, and that there ought to be "gay marriage"? The offensive nonsense of the gay activists is hard for any average person to tolerate; how can the Maker of Adam and Eve tolerate it? How can the holy and sovereign God of the universe tolerate a people that blaspheme Him in that way?

It makes sense that we would be met with God's judgment. And not merely an economic downturn every seven years; no, death and destruction. America has to be sorry and feel sorrow before anything will change. Before the light will shine in the minds of men, they have to be awakened by a traumatic event. I hope to warn as many people as possible, and save as many lives as possible. But let's not be delusional. We are dealing with darkness. We are dealing with an evil age in the history of man.

Nuclear devastation is not going to happen by accident. Its going to happen because of the sins of the people. The people have become greedy and materialistic. It seems the only meaning Americans can find in this world is a little plastic and some feel-good pleasures. What a hollow existence. We lie, we cheat, and we call it competition. Corporate leaders are eager to buy out politicians, and politicians are happy to take a bribe. Every year we hear new stories of mass shootings. And we need not go far to find gang violence alongside rampant drug use. If Americans would just look at the pitiful state we're in. Do any marriages last in America? Are there any children born with a married father and mother? Should I mention STDs? I shudder to speak of all the preborn babies that ended up in a garbage bag. What a hate-filled existence! What hypocrisy from homosexuals who claim "love" but support abortion! See through the deception for what it is: an excuse for perversion and sexual promiscuity.

This is why America must be humbled. If we are to fulfill our destiny, the wickedness must be purged from America. Anytime a person has cancer, the cancer must be removed. An athlete with a fracture must be healed before he can perform his best. Our nation is plagued with cancerous sin, limping into the 21st century with a million fractures. We could not possibly conquer the world, or even defend our own existence, with the corrupt leadership in DC, the constant stream of lies coming out of Hollywood, and cross-dressers in the Air Force! America is not a shining city on a hill today, but more like a red light district. If we want to shine, we have to purge the evil out of our midst.

I believe it would do some good to delve deeper into what is plaguing America. What I have mentioned so far is the outward symptom of a larger disease. We worship idols in America. We believe in freedom and equality, and other such things, but we have lost our faith in God. We approach each issue with blind faith in one of these ideas, yet never ask ourselves what is written in Scripture. Many Christians have even succumbed to the idea that God's word doesn't mix with politics, effectively handing our government over to Satan.

Gay activists are always trumpeting equality as their cause. If heterosexuals can marry, why not homosexuals? We might as well ask why a man can't marry his dog. But this, they argue, is all about equality. Maybe so, if we have a blind faith in the idea of equality. Then many arguments can be made to justify many different perversions, just by claiming to be "born with it". The idea of equality, without any restraint from the idea of morality, can be taken in many different directions, with many scary outcomes. Virtues such as equality and freedom are not virtuous at all, if they are divorced of morality. And a marriage of Adam and Steve, to put them on equal terms with Adam and Eve, is no less perverted and wrong. No less does it go against God's word, as well as nature. In our political debates, though, we allow no room for God or morality. We assume they have no place in politics. Equality and freedom can be esteemed the greatest virtues in politics, but any argument that begins with "its morally wrong" or "God condemns it" is cast out, as if it has no relevance whatsoever. That, my fellow American, is the disease and cancer destroying America.

What comes first? What is of the highest importance? And what can any nation be founded upon? Certain ideas like freedom and equality, or individuality and consent? Certainly, no. The beginning of man is not man, and the purpose of man is not to serve man. Man did not make himself, and man cannot sustain himself. If the law is set up to serve man, along with the ideas man holds dear, our society will end similar to any one of the horrors of history. Because the only true foundation for a society is God. Man derives his existence from God. Man's purpose on earth is to honor God. And everything that is good or bad is designated as such by God. If we try to go our own way, we will fail miserably, because we are trying to fight against God and the nature He made.

If we say men should have freedom to do what they want so long as it doesn't harm anyone else, what happens? There will be no restraint to vices such as gambling, drugs, gangs, promiscuous sex and the like. Under such circumstances, if a man doesn't ruin his finances with gambling, or his health with drugs, he may end his life by contracting HIV. Its evident that men will fill the void with something. If a person isn't living his life for Christ, he will find something else to entertain himself.

If we succumb to the deceptive arguments which deify equality, what will result from that? Where would that take us, or where has it taken us? Already gay marriage is legal in some states, and the gay activists keep pushing to make it nationally recognized. Of course then, not only will men be marrying men and women women, but gay couples will want to adopt children. They cannot have their own children naturally, because God never intended for them to even be "married", let alone have children. But they will demand it as their right, equally as much as any heterosexual couple, to adopt. And if the natural mother doesn't want her child being adopted by a gay couple (as you can imagine, many wouldn't), the gay couple will scream "discrimination!" Anything they are denied, they will claim it as discrimination. By this tactic they can practically hold the nation hostage. They can get practically anything they want by simply complaining of discrimination. But that would not be an issue if we didn't allow them to deify equality in the first place, and we held to the plain teachings of Scripture. The only real question in America should not be whether gays can marry (far from it), but what to do with those who commit the act itself. Should gay sex be punished by law? That is the only real question Americans need to consider.

All of this will come to a violent end. Not by peaceful activism, nor by violent moralists. It will come to a violent end when God Himself decides to punish America for its sins. What argument can then be made against His word, when cities are littered with radiation and corpses? Will anyone attempt to say that God's word is not relevant then? Will the highest question be one of freedom or equality? No, Americans will pray for survival at that point. Americans will hope God is real, even if they've lost all faith in Him, just because He will be our only hope of survival. But remember this: it is God who strikes us. It is God who will purge America of its evil inclinations. It is God who will kill the leaders of our present moral morass. And if anyone wants to make himself an enemy of God, now or then, he will find himself burning in that eternal lake of fire. There is, and can only be, one way to respond to God's wrath: fear. Fear Him, and submit to His word.

XVII

A new Constitution

America needs to be born again. Something must change before we could be the nation God uses to bring peace and blessing to the world. And it must change from the very foundation of America. The Constitution itself must be changed. Remember how the Eye of Providence stands atop the pyramid? Remember how the pyramid is unfinished? There is something missing from the Constitution. Something that is of the utmost importance. Nowhere does it declare God's sovereignty over this nation. Nowhere does it require the law be in accordance with God's law. Instead it speaks of "the People" as the highest authority. So if the people decide something, whatever it may be, that is the law of the land. But this ignores the fact that God is supreme over all His creation, and that His will will be done. No one can thwart the plans of God. It also implies that the people are their own god; again, another idol that Americans worship. Whatever the majority thinks, or whatever our "supreme" court decides, its taken as the gospel truth. Its taken as the highest word, but we know it isn't true. No lesser god can exist which doesn't blaspheme the holy Creator of everything. And a nation, such as the United States, whose sole purpose is to fulfill the plan of God, cannot rebel against God without paying the price. So it must be declared and made official that God is sovereign over this nation, and that no law can be made which contradicts His word.

There are two simple amendments to accomplish this:

1. An amendment stating that God is sovereign over the United States. Let it be made official. We the people do not believe ourselves to be god, nor do we think we have the right or authority to act against His will.

2. An amendment stating that no law shall be passed which contradicts the Bible. I know some people will argue against this. They will say we cannot have such an amendment, because people interpret the Bible differently. Yes, and people interpret the Constitution differently. The whole "interpret differently" argument is flawed. If we're talking about prophecy, four beasts or seven churches, then yes, we may reasonably come to different interpretations. Passages like that require interpretation, because their meaning is not plain. But when Scripture says, "love your neighbor as yourself," its meaning is very simple. He, Jesus, means exactly what He says. When He says, "do unto others as you would have them do unto you," it doesn't take an expert to figure it out. Often a child will understand these passages more readily, because a child applies a straightforward and simple approach, rather than trying to analyze Scripture. Could that be why Jesus said no one can enter the kingdom of God unless he becomes like a little child?

Since we already interpret the Constitution, and require our courts to interpret it when they make judgments regarding it, why should we not interpret the Bible? The Bible is the word of God. It is the highest word on earth. The Constitution can only come second. So why not require judges to interpret the Bible, as well as the Constitution? Why not force constitutional scholars to be biblical scholars as well? We should place the highest importance on what the Bible means, and only secondly place importance on what the Constitution means. We should require our elected officials to swear to uphold the Bible firstly, the Constitution secondly, rather than simply placing a hand on the Bible.

If America is to be born again, where might it happen? We have to go back to the place where America was born the first time. I'm not talking about DC, because that's not where America was founded, and it will be destroyed shortly. I'm not talking about NYC, because that too will be destroyed. I'm talking about another city on the east coast, which sits directly in between NYC and DC. Its where America was born. Its where the Declaration of Independence and the Constitution were written: Philadelphia, at Independence Hall. Its there, if the Constitution is to be rewritten, that it must happen. And when a new federal government is to be elected (by special election of course), it is there they will establish a new capital for the nation. Its no coincidence that this city, where both of our founding documents were written and signed, shares its name with the church of this era. The New World Order and the church in Philadelphia run concurrent with each other. It just makes sense, if a new American capital is to lead the way in establishing a New World Order, that it share its name with the church of this era. That name - Philadelphia - means the city of brotherly love. A worldwide sense of brotherly love will define this new era.

XVIII

The dawn

So what happens then? The United States is bombed, then what? We repent, then what? The capital is moved, then what? Israel is invaded by a coalition of Arab nations. The nations invading Israel are destroyed by God's wrath, then what? A third temple is built, then what? The United States conquers the world, then what? Peace. After all of these events, and after all of this turmoil, the world will finally experience peace. It is in this setting that the gospel reaches every corner of the earth. Jews are shown by miraculous events that Jesus is Messiah. Muslims are shown, by the same miraculous event, that Jesus is Messiah and God. The world converts to Christianity, at least in name, if not in soul as well.

What will it be like in this New World Order? Will it be global tyranny? No. Its not the man-made version of globalization we see in the world today, with the elites of today. It is a version of globalization which comes from God. It will not mean tyranny, but rather freedom for many oppressed peoples. Just imagine North Korea becoming the same as South Korea. That is not tyranny but freedom for Koreans. Just imagine practically every middle eastern nation being transformed into another Israel. That does not mean tyranny for Arab Muslims, but rather freedom for (then) Arab Christians.

Jerusalem will be the center of it all. It will not try to dictate the affairs of every nation and every state and every locality. It will instead establish a global Constitution, which will guarantee certain rights for individuals, and grant certain powers to each national assembly. Some laws will be universal, other laws national, and other laws local. For instance, there will be a universal ban on weapons of mass destruction. No more nuclear weapons. The need for such a global law will become abundantly clear when the US suffers the deadly affects of nuclear devastation. We cannot rely on thorough security checks; not only does that infringe upon personal freedom, it cannot entirely prevent an attack. The only way to ensure that no nuclear attack ever happens again is to ensure that no nuclear weapons exist in the world. Another example of a global law would be the requirement that every nation have a truly democratic form of government. Not that each form of government has to be exactly the same, but that every national government has to be truly democratic. These couple examples of global laws give you an idea of how Israel will lead and rule the world. The United States will follow and enforce whatever directive comes from Jerusalem. But you can be certain that it will be good, because those in power will be directly influenced by God, and directly responsible to Him. Most of the lawmaking will remain at the national, state/providential and local levels.

The end result of all this will be peace and prosperity. We see the potential for prosperity already, in the incredible advance of technology. However, technology offers two opposite possibilities: global prosperity, or global annihilation. Computers and automated manufacturing could bring global prosperity. But nuclear weapons could bring global annihilation. The difference lies in the question of peace or war. If there's peace in the world, there will be global prosperity. But if the world descends into war, it will likely mean global annihilation. As you know, I believe peace is what will actually happen. This is the dawn that I speak of. A new day, a new era, a New World Order. A world that is Christian, as well as peaceful and prosperous.

Getting back to the seven churches, we see how this aligns with their prophecies. The church in Philadelphia is blessed in such a way that the synagogue of Satan must recognize it; so it is an outward blessing. Peace and prosperity are outward blessings, in addition to the fact that persecuted Christians will be moved to the heads of every nation. These will be the most respected people in every nation. Respected first for their wisdom, because they were proven correct. And secondly because Jerusalem sides with them. World leaders will make sure that those who were Christians before the great event - the war of Gog - are given preferential treatment after it; especially those who suffered persecution before it. It is fulfillment of the promise Jesus gives to the church in Philadelphia.

XIX

The end

Finally, we have the church in Laodicea. It is the last of the seven churches. It is the church of the last days. They say they are rich; in physical possessions, they are. But their spiritual reality is "wretched, pitiful, poor, blind and naked". Let's follow the progression from the church in Philadelphia to the church in Laodicea. If we want to know how long it is, from the emerging of the church in Philadelphia (now) to the fulfillment of the church in Laodicea, we only have to look at the 70 sevens prophecy in Daniel 9. If you remember, the decree to rebuild and restore Jerusalem happened in 1969. From then till the year Jesus returns, it speaks of 490 years (7 sevens plus 62 sevens plus one seven). That puts the return of Christ at about the year 2459 (please excuse me, Future Generations, if its not exactly that year). But the time frame is correct for placing both Philadelphia and Laodicea into our timeline. It is roughly 400 more years: about 300 more years for the age of Philadelphia, and about 100 years for the age of Laodicea. Why do I divide the years that way? It actually gives some symmetry to the whole timeline of the seven churches. Ephesus was about 100 years, and Smyrna was almost 300 years. Plus it makes logical sense, when considering how things will likely progress.

We know that the age of Philadelphia, in which there is a global New World Order (led by the nation of Israel), will yield peace and prosperity. So we need no explanation as to why the church in Laodicea calls themselves rich (and foolishly think, because of their wealth, they don't need God). At the time that Laodicea emerges the world will have grown very wealthy, being the result of peace and the advance of technology. We also know that wealth tends to weaken a person's faith. As Jesus said, you cannot serve both God and money. As Paul said, the love of money is the root of all evil. And Jesus said, wherever your treasure is, there your heart will be also. So you cannot have wealth without loving wealth, at least to some degree. And the longer you have wealth, the more you will fall in love with it. It is no mystery then, as to why Jesus calls them wretched and pitiful and blind. The wealth has made them so. Let us remember this (and let future generations take note): *Though physical blessing may seem like a blessing in the short term, it is a curse in the long term.* Never let physical possession come between you and God. And never let it come between you and loving your neighbor. The life of a persecuted martyr is better than the life of a rich man. Blessed are the poor, Jesus says, and woe to those who are rich.

Now we see the stage set for the great apostasy. The church in Laodicea emerges in the last hundred years. They are rich physically, but poor spiritually. Their spiritual poverty opens the door to all of the evil things that Paul describes in 2Timothy 3: "But mark this: There will be terrible times in the last days. People will be lovers of themselves, lovers of money, boastful, proud, abusive, disobedient to their parents, ungrateful, unholy, without love, unforgiving, slanderous, without self-control, brutal, not lovers of the good, treacherous, rash, conceited, lovers of pleasure rather than lovers of God." We see some of it today, but it will be far worse in the last days.

Let's take note of a few things while we're on the subject of the churches and last days. Only the last three churches have any mention of the return of Christ. In the letter to Sardis, Jesus warns that He will return like a thief in the night, if they do not wake up and do the works He requires. In the letter to Philadelphia He promises to keep them from the hour of trial that is about to come upon the whole world. What could that be, but the tribulation period? In that verse you may actually have a hint of a rapture (for those who like to think there will be a rapture). And in the letter to Laodicea He says He is about to spit them out of his mouth. This means He is about to kick them out of the kingdom. It happens by their denial of Him. Lukewarm Christians can superficially claim Christ, while in their hearts they don't care. But when someone holds a gun to their head (or however it might happen), then they will be forced to admit what is true: they will deny Christ. Those who wish to stay in the kingdom will have to die a martyr's death. But it is as Jesus said, those who try to save their lives with lose them, and those who lose their lives for Him will have eternal life. Since the vast majority of those in the Laodicean church will try to save their lives, they will be "spat out" when they deny His name.

All of the rest you already know. There is a seven year tribulation period. The Antichrist rules during this time. The False Prophet speaks on behalf of the Antichrist and performs many signs. There are two witnesses in the temple, who preach against the wickedness for 42 months (3 and 1/2 years). The False Prophet kills the two witnesses, but they resurrect and ascend into heaven. All of it culminates with plagues and the battle of Armageddon. Jesus returns to the earth, and a thousand year period of peace and prosperity ensues. It is no coincidence that this thousand years (the millennial reign of

Christ) begins with the conquest of a white horseman as well (Revelation 19). But this White Horseman establishes a perfect peace, and His rule over the earth is ironclad. As the Scripture says, He will rule the nations with an iron scepter. There is the main difference. The first white horseman (the US) establishes a relative peace on earth. The second White Horseman (Jesus) establishes a perfect peace on earth. And the thousand years ends with one final rebellion, followed by the New Jerusalem.

XX

Conclusion

If we're going to interpret biblical prophecy honestly, we have to take the whole together, rather than each one separately. The tendency of some is to treat each prophecy as its own separate thing. But I believe I've shown, the best way to interpret prophecy is one prophecy in connection with every prophecy. Each prophecy adds to the context of every other prophecy, since they all relate to the same world and the same timeline. It is absolutely necessary that they fit together.

What you may have noticed about this book is that every interpretation does fit together, and they intertwine. We have looked at prophecies in Daniel, Isaiah, Ezekiel, Zechariah, the words of Jesus in the gospels, the words of Paul, and of course Revelation. We have been all over the Bible, and have touched on many different subjects. But if you take every one of these prophecies and put them on a timeline, they each have their own spot, and none of them are in contradiction with the others. They even make for a very sensible timeline of events. For example, we have the prophecy of the leopard beast, and the fulfillment of the fourth wing of it, in a Fourth Reich that will rise to power this decade. And we know, if our interpretation of the prophecy concerning the white horseman is true, then the fulfillment of the fourth wing of the leopard beast will happen soon, or never at all. Because it won't be very long until the white horseman has conquered the world, eliminating any possibility of a Fourth Reich. And yet there is ample time for the rise, and the fall, of a Fourth Reich, before the fulfillment of the white horseman comes to pass.

(As a side note, if you pay attention to Europe, you'll notice a rise in neo-Nazi political organizations and nationalistic sentiment, which is an indication of things to come).

For another example, we can reason that the world will not become rich if there continues to be war. But if our interpretation of the church in Laodicea is correct, then the world will be rich in the last days. And our interpretation of the white horseman shows us how. It will conquer the world and thereby bring about peace, just like Octavian and the Pax Romana; conquest results in peace. And if any should doubt that the white horseman must bring about peace, we point them to the prophecy concerning the red horseman, who "takes peace from the earth". If the century before Jesus returns enjoys peace (until the red horseman, that is), then its reasonable to think that it will enjoy prosperity as well; perfectly consistent with our interpretation of Laodicea.

I can go on and on with examples. The seven churches themselves fit together perfectly in chronological sequence. I already mentioned the fact that its only the last three which allude to Jesus' return. But it seems as if something in each letter indicates the transition to the next church. From Ephesus to Pergamum, the church starts by holding to a strict orthodoxy, then progresses to a more heretical mix of doctrines. From Smyrna to Pergamum, we see that the persecution Smyrna suffered is somewhat lingering in Pergamum. From Pergamum to Thyatira, we see that the false doctrines and false practices progress, until they come under the direction of "Jezebel". And since Sardis does not tolerate the woman Jezebel like Thyatira, it makes sense that there would be a sharp break between Thyatira and Sardis. Thus the Protestant Reformation, and the sharp distinction between Catholic and Protestant. From Sardis to Philadelphia, we see that Sardis' growing weakness has resulted in Philadephia's weakness (Jesus says to Sardis, "strengthen what remains," and to Philadelphia, "I know you have little strength"). And from Philadelphia to Laodicea, we see the result of God's blessing towards Philadelphia. The outward physical blessing is carried forward so that the church in Laodicea is wealthy. Each one of the churches, as you can see, is a natural progression from the previous to the next.

The conclusion of this book is very straightforward. The immediate purpose of it is to warn people. There are four different groups who can take a warning from this book.

1. Catholics who are close to the Vatican can be warned, if they see the rise of a Fourth Reich. Its best to distance yourself from the woman Jezebel, the Vatican. I know Catholics won't want to hear it, and won't want to believe it, but its the truth. The Vatican is a false prophet, and God will judge her for her sins.

2. Middle-eastern Muslims can take a warning from this book: do not involve yourself in any war against Israel. Ezekiel 38 and 39 prophesies a major judgment against the enemies who come against Israel. Anyone in the middle east who heeds this warning will avoid war with Israel at all costs, and pray to God for protection.

3. Israel can take a warning from this book. When the war of Gog breaks out, there's going to be a massive earthquake in

Israel. When you see a coalition of nations coming against you, know that the time is near. Do not be afraid of the advancing armies, but prepare yourself for an earthquake unlike any the world has seen. Especially get out of every building.

4. Americans can take a warning from this book. Especially those who live in New York City, or Washington DC, or Los Angeles: move. Get out of the city. Even if it doesn't happen on the 7th of September, still proceed with caution. I cannot be absolutely certain that the 7th is the exact day it will happen. But it does seem that it must happen sometime around then (September, 2015). It could even be the 11th again. The best plan of action is simply to avoid those cities at least during the months of August and September. If November rolls around and nothing has happened, I will gladly concede that I was completely wrong and sigh with relief.

For a few concluding remarks, I say: Always keep God's word near to your head and heart. Study everything I have pointed out to you. Question it, scrutinize it. But whatever the future holds, your future can only be bright if you faithfully serve Christ. So always remember Him and His word. He commands the church in Philadelphia to patiently endure. And that's the key to a Christian life. It is an endurance race. We must keep running. We must keep going, keep our heads up, and always remember Him. The longer we can endure, the longer the world will enjoy peace and love. Imagine a world in which there is no abortion, no war and very little crime. Imagine if every famine were responded to immediately by a global response team, and not one single person died of hunger. Imagine if the whole world pitched in to help a nation which has suffered from a natural disaster. Imagine such a world filled with love and peace.

Imagine a world where even the poorest have all the basics of life. Its very possible! And its something worth fighting for. Finally, Jesus prays, "your kingdom come, your will be done, on earth as it is in heaven." Christianity is not about waiting to go to heaven. It is about bringing heaven down to earth. Jesus prays for God's kingdom to come, and for His will to be done, on *earth*. That is your mission, Christian: bring heaven down to earth.

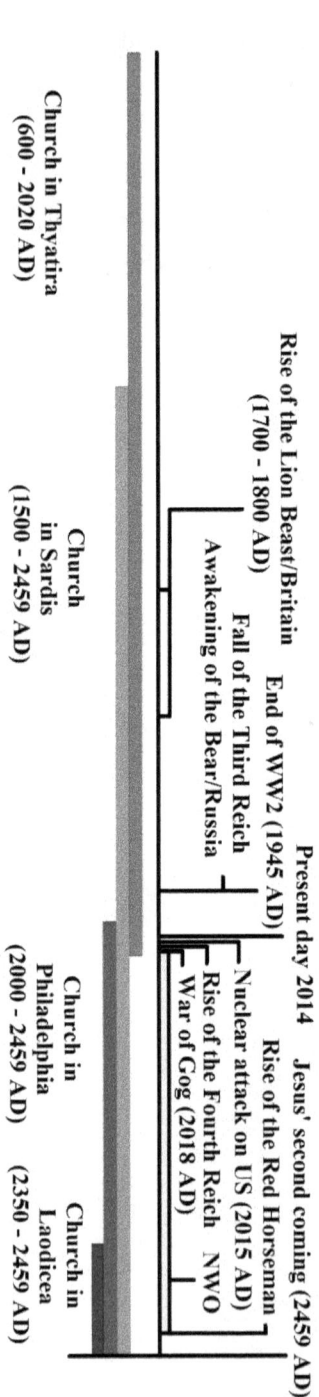
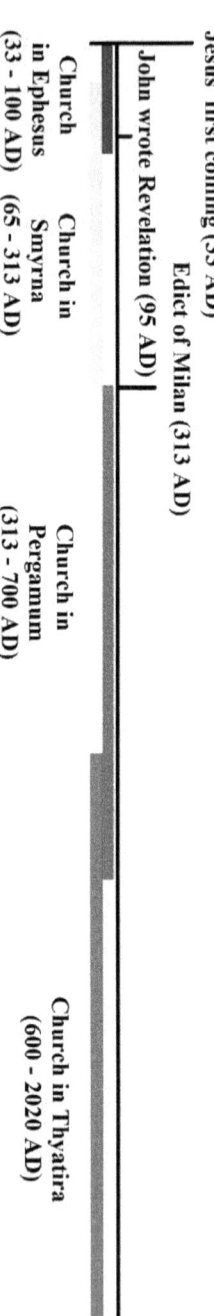

www.ingramcontent.com/pod-product-compliance
Lightning Source LLC
Chambersburg PA
CBHW071303040426
42444CB00009B/1845